PLAYING THE
LANGUAGE GAME

Open University Press

English, Language, and Education series

General Editor: Anthony Adams
Lecturer in Education, University of Cambridge

TITLES IN THE SERIES

Narrative and Argument
Richard Andrews (ed.)

The Problem with Poetry
Richard Andrews

Writing Development
Roslyn Arnold

Writing Policy in Action
Eve Bearne and Cath Farrow

Secondary Worlds
Michael Benton

Time for Drama
Roma Burgess and Pamela Gaudry

Readers, Texts, Teachers
Bill Corcoran and Emrys Evans (eds)

Thinking Through English
Paddy Creber

Teaching Secondary English
David Curtis

Developing English
Peter Dougill (ed.)

Reading against Racism
Emrys Evans

Children Talk About Books
Donald Fry

English Teaching and Media Education
Andrew Goodwyn

English at the Core
Peter Griffith

Literary Theory and English Teaching
Peter Griffith

Lesbian and Gay Issues in the English Classroom
Simon Harris

Reading and Response
Mike Hayhoe and Stephen Parker (eds)

Assessing English
Brian Johnston

Lipservice: The Story of Talk in Schools
Pat Jones

Language and the English Curriculum
John Keen

Shakespeare in the Classroom
Susan Leach

Oracy Matters
Margaret MacLure, Terry Phillips and
Andrew Wilkinson (eds)

Language Awareness for Teachers
Bill Mittins

Beginning Writing
John Nichols *et al.*

Teaching Literature for Examinations
Robert Protherough

Developing Response to Fiction
Robert Protherough

The Making of English Teachers
Robert Protherough and Judith Atkinson

Young People Reading
Charles Sarland

English Teaching from A–Z
Wayne Sawyer, Anthony Adams and
Ken Watson

Reconstructing 'A' Level English
Patrick Scott

School Writing
Yanina Sheeran and Douglas Barnes

Playing the Language Game
Valerie Shepherd

Reading Narrative as Literature
Andrew Stibbs

Collaboration and Writing
Morag Styles (ed.)

Reading Within and Beyond the Classroom
Dan Taverner

Reading for Real
Barrie Wade (ed.)

The Quality of Writing
Andrew Wilkinson

The Writing of Writing
Andrew Wilkinson (ed.)

Spoken English Illuminated
Andrew Wilkinson, Alan Davies and
Deborah Berrill

PLAYING THE LANGUAGE GAME

Valerie Shepherd

Open University Press
Buckingham • Philadelphia

Open University Press
Celtic Court
22 Ballmoor
Buckingham
MK18 1XW

and

1900 Frost Road, Suite 101
Bristol, PA 19007, USA

First Published 1993

A catalogue record of this book is available from the British Library

Library of Congress Cataloging-in-Publication Data

Shepherd, Valerie.
    Playing the language game/Valerie Shepherd.
      p. cm. – (English, language, and education)
    Includes bibliographical references (p.) and index.
    ISBN 0–335–09939–4
    1. Language and languages. I. Title. II. Series: English,
language, and education series.
    P106.S535 1993
    400—dc20   92-18668
                                        CIP

Typeset by Graphicraft Typesetters, Ltd, Hong Kong
Printed in Great Britain by Biddles Ltd, Guildford and Kings Lynn

Contents

General editor's introduction

The present volume in the *English, Language, and Education* series originated in an unusual context. Just over a year ago I took part in a conference at Nottingham Polytechnic on Industry and the Arts. One of the workshops at that conference, which I attended, was conducted by Valerie Shepherd who demonstrated the ways in which she was helping student teachers to come to terms with linguistic ideas, as proposed in the Kingman Inquiry, by playing a series of 'language games'. We, in fact, played one of these games (**Talking Power** (2.3) in the present volume), and it struck me at once that there was potential material for a book here. Consequently I encouraged Valerie to develop further the first draft of what had begun as an informal handbook of games, mainly for internal use in her institution, and also asked her to explore whether the games could also be developed in such a way as to enable them to be used with younger school-students. The present volume represents the fruits of her labours in these areas.

None the less, I had no idea at the time quite how the book would turn out. I had expected a practical 'gamester's' guide to language and this has certainly been part of the product. But what I had not expected was the sheer quantity of linguistic knowledge and understanding that the book would also contain, the discussion ranging across the elements and structures of language to their use in a variety of cultural and social contexts.

Since the publication of the Report of the Kingman Inquiry and the establishment of Knowledge about Language as an important dimension within the National Curriculum in the UK, teachers have become much more aware of their responsibilities for this vital area of work. However, given the nature of the previous training of many of those currently in post in our schools, the need to do something about language is often perceived as a vague kind of guilt feeling rather than as something about which anything practical can be done. Several earlier volumes in this series, notably Keen (1992) and Mittins (1990), have gone some way towards giving teachers the knowledge needed to fulfil their responsibilities under the language requirements of the National

Curriculum. However, Valerie Shepherd has gone a significant step beyond this in providing an entertaining methodology for teaching both teachers and students about language and how it works in a coherently planned and organized way.

The method essentially relies upon a series of role play type simulations that enable students, of whatever age, to play the part of field linguisticians and, through so doing, observe and speculate upon language in action in all its forms and variety. In so doing they will come to have not just a series of intellectual insights into language but also an affective understanding of its effects. The last attempt to introduce work of this kind into the classroom was the pioneering *Language in Use* project of the early 1970s which attempted to provide teachers with a framework for teaching in which they could explore with their classes some of the insights of sociolinguistics, influenced especially by the work of M.A.K. Halliday. However, *Language in Use* suffered from the same problem as much pioneering work of its time – it underestimated the amount that teachers needed to know about language and did not give them sufficient help over the pedagogy required to put its principles into action. It became therefore one of the most bought and talked about and one of the least used books of its time. None the less its influence on the future development of English studies has been considerable and it is doubtful whether the present volume would exist if *Language in Use* had not preceded it.

Now, however, post-Kingman we are in a much better position to under-stand the need for systematic attention to work in language for all teachers in training though, in general, we have yet to see the implementation of the frequently repeated suggestion that there should be some elements in language study common to all courses for intending teachers of language, whether they be English or Modern Languages specialists. Valerie Shepherd's work at Nottingham grew directly out of a need to create a course of this kind for her own students and to 'sell' to them the idea of language being important by making it fun as well as intellectually stimulating to learn about.

The idea that language is a game people play is of course an old one which has been interpreted by numerous writers with varying degrees of scholarship and seriousness. The present volume combines both these qualities with a clear understanding of the practicalities of the classrooms in which the Games are to be played. Most of them require little or no preparation except that of the mind of the teacher who is going to lead the pupils to get the most out of playing the various Games. The volume is thus much easier to use in the everyday life of the classroom than *Language in Use* proved to be. I believe that the reader will find the arrangement of the Games and the instructions for how to play them logically organized and easy to use.

In my own reading of the book I have particularly enjoyed the Afterwords which give an authentic feel of how the Games worked in practice with the very different groups with which they have been trialled. I have also learned a great deal that was new to me and been reminded of much that I had read elsewhere but forgotten.

At the time that this volume is being prepared for the press it has just been announced that there is to be a review of the requirements for the English National Curriculum in England and Wales. The terms under which this review has been proposed suggest that there will be even more public confusion than at present over such issues as the role of Standard English inside and outside the classroom and its perceived relationship to Received Pronunciation. In this context, so far as both teachers and their students are concerned, it becomes even more important to clear up misconceptions by stressing the need for Knowledge about Language. Thus the present volume is even more timely than we had anticipated. It will be published at the very time when the debate over language in the curriculum, already a political hot potato, will be at its height. Therefore, the book will retain its usefulness in the context of curriculum change and through the kind of programme it recommends, students will be encouraged to understand and manage their linguistic competence.

All of us, including the youngest children (see M.A.K. Halliday's own discussion of this in *Learning How to Mean*, 1975), spend most of our lives intuitively 'playing the language game'. It is, therefore, just as well for us to understand the 'rules' by which we, and others, play this game so that we can do so more effectively. Valerie Shepherd's present offering is a signally original contribution in that direction which should help us all to be both better and more understanding players of what is itself one of the most important of life's many and varied games.

Anthony Adams

Acknowledgements

I am grateful to the Enterprise Initiative in Higher Education at The Nottingham Trent University, particularly its co-ordinator Lynne Hapgood, for supporting the development of language games.

Special thanks are due to schools and colleges, staff and students, who experimented with the Games. These included the English Departments of Charles Keene College of Further Education, Leicester; King Edward VII Community College, Coalville, Leicestershire; Tupton Hall School, Old Tupton, Chesterfield, Derbyshire; PGCE students at Loughborough University; Dr Margaret Sheil of the English Department, State University of New York at Oneonta; undergraduate, Lucy Shepherd; The Nottingham Trent University colleague, Elizabeth Morrish, and, especially, The Nottingham Trent University students who were in their first or second year of Communication or Education studies during 1990 and 1991. All made constructive criticisms and offered invaluable suggestions (which are included in the Afterword to each Game) and some provided additional games. However, I am solely responsible for any errors or over-simplifications which may have occurred in the book's introduction to aspects of linguistic theory. I should also like to thank the audio-visual team in The Nottingham Trent University Faculty of Humanities who provided invaluable assistance with project work.

I am grateful to Emmett Williams for allowing me to reproduce his poem 'do you remember'. e.e. cummings's poem 'Buffalo Bill's' and extracts from 'anyone lived in a pretty how town', are reproduced by permission of MacGibbon and Kee, an imprint of HarperCollins Publishers Ltd (UK); and are reprinted from COMPLETE POEMS, 1913–1962, by e.e. cummings, by permission of Liveright Publishing Corporation. Copyright © 1923, 1925, 1931, 1935, 1938, 1939, 1940, 1944, 1945, 1946, 1947, 1948, 1949, 1950, 1951, 1952, 1953, 1954, 1955, 1956, 1957, 1958, 1959, 1960, 1961, 1962 by the Trustees for the e.e. cummings Trust. Copyright © 1961, 1963, 1968 by Marion Morehouse Cummings.

Finally, thanks may be due to people I do not know but whose ideas I could have unwittingly borrowed without acknowledgement. I believe the Games are largely original, but I am aware that in the thousands of classrooms where language is being taught several great minds may well have thought alike.

1 Learning about language

From parsing to practice

Language is *behaviour*: vital, creative and powerful. Discussion, argument, instruction; the writing of poetry, drama, polemic, prayer; lying, cheating, teasing, joking; all these have little to do with the dry, dreary exercise of grammatical analysis for its own sake, with the labelling of parts, the dissection of clauses. No wonder the classrooms of the 1960s and 1970s abandoned the learning of language by narrow, prescriptive rule and rote. Merely knowing that an 'adjective is a describing word' and being able to spot one at fifty paces appeared to do little for children's language behaviour, its confidence, its creativity or its clarity.

Moreover, as an educationalist rightly remarked in the 1960s (Flower 1966: 26):

> We learn to skate on the ice and to swim in the water, not in the class room.
> Similarly we learn to speak and write our mother tongue in the full context of our
> daily usage . . .

The stimulus of an ordinary language environment, the buzz of everyday talk, is vital to the development of language.

However, there is no reason why this linguistic environment, unlike the ice rink or the swimming pool, cannot be brought into the classroom in order to encourage further development in language skills. Indeed, experiential language learning did enter the school rooms of the 1960s through a wide range of language activities like those suggested by the *Language in Use* project (1969 and 1971).

Now, traffic notices, instruction manuals, magazines and newspapers were worked on in the classroom. And the spoken word, largely ignored in the days of parsing, received a share of attention as pupils were encouraged to think about the language of football crowds, of weather forecasts, of interviews, speeches, sermons, prayers, and so on. For the initiators of *Language in Use* rightly argued that children bring to school an 'extensive knowledge' of language. Therefore, their teaching methods would 'start from that native intuition' (Doughty *et al.* 1971: 9).

In this respect, *Language in Use* endorsed the linguist M.A.K. Halliday's view of children's understanding of language, a view expressed in his paper, 'Relevant models of language' (1973: 7–21). 'Models', for Halliday, are our images of language arising out of its uses:

> The child's understanding of what language is derived from his own experience of language in situations of use . . . [his models therefore include] the instrumental, the regulatory, the interactional, the personal, the heuristic, the imaginative and the representational. Each of these is his interpretation of a function of language with which he is familiar.
>
> (Halliday 1973: 17)

Adults, on the other hand, though we share all these functions, may be conscious only of the 'representational' model, the use of language to express propositions, to refer and inform. From the point of view of the child, this is a very inadequate model. Much more is needed in the classroom.

> A minimum requirement for an educationally relevant approach to language is that it takes account of the child's own linguistic experience, defining this experience in terms of its richest potential . . .
>
> (Halliday 1973: 19)

The *Language in Use* project aimed to do just this and the full range of a child's 'models' of language potential was encouraged in classrooms from the 1960s onwards. However, although the project intended children to 'work towards a much more developed awareness of the part which language plays in the lives of men and society, and the means it has for playing it' (Doughty *et al.* 1971: 9), explicit understanding of those means was not, in practice, encouraged. The pendulum had swung so far from the old style parsing that it was argued:

> What the teacher could tell [students] about English is not likely to affect their practice of the language or their understanding of what is said to them. His role does not resemble that of the physics or geography specialist but rather the activity of the cricket coach . . .
>
> (Flower 1966: 26)

But this is a misleading point of view (and not, as explained below, entirely endorsed by *Language in Use*). It misrepresents the language teacher and also the sports coach. After all, the latter's role is, by definition, to coach – not only through encouraging practice but also by *commenting upon* the stance, the grip, the movement of batsman, bowler and fielder with the intention of improving their performance. Moreover, there is no reason why commentary upon language, its sounds, words, structures and their patterns of use, should be any more inhibiting than judicious commentary on sports practice – so long as that commentary is linked, unlike the old method of parsing, to the real-life contexts of human behaviour.

Indeed, commentary can have a liberating, enhancing effect. So, *Playing the Language Game* blends two approaches to language, borrowing something of the old analytical method but widening its scope, giving it relevance, by relating analysis in some meaningful way to language in the contexts of actual human behaviour. That is, as the Kingman Report of the Committee of Inquiry into the Teaching of English Language (1988) recommended, and subsequent curriculum directives and examination syllabuses require, pupils are helped to make *explicit* their implicit understanding of language in use: in effect, *to do linguistics*.

Living with linguistics: From description to critical insight

How, precisely, might this 'making explicit', this doing linguistics, work – and (for the phrase has a ring of the formality that, together with restrictive, old-fashioned parsing, was rejected long ago) to what liberating purpose? To a large extent, as all teaching in the tradition of *Language in Use* emphasizes, we live by language. Linguistics has a role to play as a life-support system.

It can lead, via *description* and *analysis*, to the *critical explanation* of language behaviour in relation to its human contexts. However, although insights achieved in this way can result in more effective language use and response, it is important to stress that 'critical explanation' is not based on a narrowly judgemental approach, dependent on prescriptive standards.

For example, pupils might be told they are to imagine a road accident in which a well-known local person has knocked down an elderly couple. Then, they could be given two headlines which refer to the incident and which apparently come from different papers. For instance:

(a) Local dentist knocks down couple.

(b) Elderly couple knocked down.

The class would be asked to describe the language used, analysing the two headlines through comparing and contrasting their descriptions. In this respect, they would be doing something very similar to the old style language analysis, for they would need to comment on the structure of the headlines, noting for example two nouns in (a) but only one in (b), an adjective beginning both (a) and (b) and a marked difference in the syntax of the two, since (a) is an active structure and (b) a passive.

If the work stopped here, the pupils of the mid-twentieth-century class might have scored full marks. But in reality the job is only half done. For there is little point in describing language – in the old-fashioned parsing way – without analysing and explaining the description. Today's students need not only to describe language choices and how they may differ, but also, and most importantly, to relate these differences, explicitly, to their human causes and consequences.

The consequences in the case of the headlines could be crucial, for their language choices can pave the way for totally differently focused accounts of the same event – totally different interpretations of the same reality. The syntactic active/passive contrast, for instance, is hightly significant in this context.

Active sentences bring the 'actor' into the spotlight, often placing him or her prominently at the beginning of a sentence and leaving whatever or whoever has been acted upon – the 'victim' or maybe the 'beneficiary' of the act – to be mentioned later. So, placed last in (a), the couple are not specially noticeable, particularly as there are no adjectives helping readers to visualize them. But the dentist comes first – first in structure and so first to our attention – and an adjective pinpoints him or her as someone local. Do we actually *know* this puller of teeth, this terrorizer of old people?

The other headline does not invite such fascinating speculation: it seems more concerned with arousing our sympathy for the injured than our instincts for scandal. For the passive form of the headline (b) makes the couple take the foreground (and we have an adjective to help us know them, give them identities). But the person who caused the accident to the pair is not even mentioned, for passive structures give us the option to include, or to leave out, a phrase which would indicate by whom the action was perpetrated.

It is important to give this syntactic difference its full evaluative weight, recognizing its range of possible causes and consequences within and beyond the contexts of newspaper reporting. For, as Games in this book (particularly those in Chapter 3, Section 1) demonstrate, we know – more or less unconsciously – all about the potential for choosing our words and structures powerfully. Without conscious deliberation we can pick actives to pin blame on people, or to show off our own prowess; we can choose passives in order to avoid responsibility, or to spotlight our role as a badly treated victim in need of care and protection. However, as a number of the Games also show, we do not always choose: our language behaviour is often determined and circumscribed. The forces of its limitation are profound and complex. But if we know this, consciously, and can recognize the precise manifestations of determinism and relate them to their sources, then there is a greater possibility of making and controlling our own choices effectively and intelligently – and of recognizing and dealing with the language behaviour, by no means always benign, that is directed towards us. Mike Torbe (quoted in Scott 1989: 47) is right when he insists that we should:

> . . . put into our pupils' hands the ability to control their environments by giving them *insights* into language interactions . . . [in so doing we] give our pupils power over their language, and therefore over the situations in which that language is used . . . (emphasis added)

This is precisely the attitude of the Kingman Report of the Committee of Inquiry into the Teaching of English Language, which argues that language:

> ... expresses identity, enables co-operation, and confers freedom ... People need expertise in language to be able to participate effectively in a democracy ... [language power is also needed to] ease the way in those humdrum passages of life where tax returns, mortgage agreements, insurance claims are to be completed ... Competence in language is essential to competence in any job ...
>
> (1988: 7–8)

As Kingman notes, these are *adult* needs, and Professor Henry Widdowson, in an appendix to the Report, stresses his concern that the relationship of language teaching in school to use of language in later life should be made clear. Halliday (1973: 20) had also urged that school language teaching should have 'relevance to the experiences that the child will have later on'. In achieving this very necessary goal, however, the young person's current language functions are also, inevitably, addressed and enriched. For adult linguistic needs are generally a development of those varied 'models' of language which Halliday explained are at some level understood and practised in earlier years.

For instance, the linguistic construction of identity is, as Halliday's discussion of the child's 'personal' function or model of language makes clear, hardly a matter for adulthood alone. And the making, breaking and manipulating of relationships through discourse (Halliday's 'interactional' function) is not delayed until adulthood. Moreover, mixed-race and mixed-gender classes are a fact of life for children: the tensions of linguistic difference (or, rather of *attitudes* to those differences) are encountered well before they are grown up. Clearly, then, explicit language knowledge, and considered practice in its application, are vital in advance of school leaving, for life inside and outside the classroom. And several of the Games in this volume invite students to consider – to experiment with and then to explicitly describe, analyse and explain – the language of experiences that are encountered during school days and that will continue their challenge into adult life.

For example, the Game, **Language for Living** (1.8), practises, and then discusses, our everyday use of metaphor and the part it plays in the construction of our lives: What, for instance, has our response to AIDS got to do with metaphor? Then, **Talking Power** (2.3) wonders whether – or not – women are disadvantaged through language resources and language use, resources and uses which the Game brings into play. **Cross Talk** (2.4) draws attention to the misunderstandings that can arise from the contrasts in different cultures' uses of language.

It is therefore clear that learning about language – doing, in effect, linguistics – is not restricted to the English class. It has an interdisciplinary relevance and can benefit from interdisciplinary input. Careful language description and analysis has a part to play in, say, sociology, psychology, history, politics and so on, whilst expertise from a wide variety of disciplines may be brought to bear on language work itself. *Playing the Language Game* takes this two-way process into account, and although the Games can be played without very considerable interdisciplinary knowledge, their applications could be further extended by specialists from a number of fields.

Teaching language

Naturally, younger pupils will not be ready to make the delicate descriptions and the more complex linguistic analyses of the older student. Nor will they be able to identify and explain, with the help of specialists where necessary, the social, psychological or political links of the language under their scrutiny. But, as they practise examining language in use, they should become sensitive to its powerful potential and, also, gradually acquainted with a *metalanguage* that will help more sophisticated language work at a later date.

This metalanguage – a language for talking and writing about language – is not jargon, used merely for its own impressive-sounding sake. On the contrary, it is a facilitator, enabling the clear and precise description, and discussion, of language behaviour. And it is not a facilitator belonging only to the teacher. Kingman (1988: 34) writes:

> . . . it will not be sufficient for the teacher alone to be aware of the formal and functional characteristics of different types of language use: the pupils must share this knowledge so that they can use it in developing their own and one another's competence.

They will be better able to support and extend each other's competence if they are fluent in the language of linguistics.

For example, maybe there is a storm, and the children are talking and writing about the fierceness of the weather. Perhaps someone says 'The rain is *hitting* the playground and the thunder keeps *banging* and *cracking*.' The sentence provides an opportunity for young children to simply recognize and label as *verbs* those words that pinpoint the action. But it could introduce older children to the difference between *transitives* and *intransitives*, the rain doing something to the playground as it hits it, the thunder keeping its activities to itself. This increasingly delicate metalanguage would then be held in readiness for the more complex stylistic analyses and explanations of older students. For instance, the writing and reading or texts in which responsibility and agency are fundamental (the narratives of art and of everyday use, say, but also of minutes, or business reports) would be facilitated by a critical understanding of their structuring through this kind of syntactic choice.

But, in order to guide this sort of work, staff will need to have more than a smattering of linguistic knowledge and its terminology. Yet, since the rejection of parsing, teacher training in linguistics has been regarded with some ambivalence.

Although *Language in Use* (1969 and 1971) had encouraged language behaviour, it had also acknowledged a relationship with linguistics.

The theme structure of *Language in Use* . . . enables the teacher to see how work in exploring language can be related back to the basic findings of Linguistic Science.

(Doughty *et al.* 1971: 11)

However, at the same time, its authors had minimized that relationship:

. . . the English teacher . . . is unlikely to find the central concern of the specialist in Linguistics, the explicit, formal and analytical description of the patterns of a language, immediately relevant to his needs.

(Doughty *et al.* 1971: 11)

There was a similar ambivalence in the Bullock Report of 1975. Its Recommendation 133 argued that linguistics has 'a considerable contribution to make to the teaching of English', but *A Language for Life* went on to wonder if it matters 'to anyone but a grammarian how you define a noun, or what the transformational rules are for forming the passive voice?' (1975: 174).

This point of view has lingered on with a 'widespread and vigorous rejection of grammatical analysis' (*English from 4 to 16: The Responses to Curriculum Matters 1*, quoted in Kingman 1988: 3). Yet how, without the knowledge and metalanguage needed to describe patterns of language, could staff and students do as *Language in Use* required and identify in its exercise on reading the news – with any useful degree of precision – 'what use of words and phrases seems to characterise the way of speaking chosen?' (Doughty *et al.* 1971: 53). How, in examining the language of crowds (1971: 223–34) could they describe 'the kinds of linguistic expression *not* used'? As for the transformational rule which the Bullock Report found irrelevant, the brief example of newspaper headline work given in this chapter depends for its insights upon an explicit if limited knowledge of related syntactic matters.

Knowing about these and other aspects of language – phonological, lexical, syntactic or semantic – for their own sake may only be of interest to the specialist linguist. But knowing in order to *apply* the knowledge is a different matter.

Therefore, in order to assist staff who are not language specialists, the Games do not stop at the play itself. Instead they include, in 'The Point of the Game', detailed notes about the related linguistic knowledge and techniques needed to help students reflect critically upon the behaviour they experience while playing. Indeed, teachers and trainee teachers have sometimes found it useful to play the Games themselves, afterwards debating their 'Point', in order to refine their own linguistic understanding. Every Game refers to related reading, so staff and pupils can take its material further if they wish (and this is likely, since *Playing the Language Game* has space to cover only a limited range of linguistic issues) but each 'Point of the Game' explains its own language essentials.

However, these 'essentials' are exploratory, revelatory and provocative, rather than prescriptive. Prescription – the insistence on certain very limited, 'right' and 'wrong', ways of looking at language, without consideration of alternative possibilities – left the classroom with the old-fashioned training in parsing and has no part to play in the linguist's description, analysis and explanation of language.

Getting it 'right': Prescription and standards

Whilst teachers and pupils may have found the demise of prescriptive parsing a relief, the general public – or at least its spokespersons – have been less than delighted. Norman Tebbitt has apparently insisted (BBC Radio 4, November 1985, see Bain 1991) that a lack of grammar teaching is the first step on a road to crime!

His opinion may be misguided, but it is hardly surprising. The powerful and prestigious have always assumed, from the Middle Ages onwards, that theirs is the best English and consequently have prescribed it for everyone else. So, rounded RP vowels, together with Standard syntax and lexicon, have rung out in the bastions of power, the church, the services (officer class) and the BBC. And some real-life Eliza Doolittles have actually 'got it', known how to use it, and become Fair Ladies of the upper classes.

And yet, by the 1930s, an examination paper was asking trainee teachers to discuss the effect of the 'uneducated' upon 'our language' (quoted in Shepherd 1990: 37). Much more recently, Prince Charles was heard to declare that the people in his office 'can't speak English properly, they can't write English properly' and to complain that he had to correct his secretaries' letters because – in his opinion – 'English is taught so bloody badly' (quoted in *Daily Mail*, 29 June 1989). It would appear that not everyone has swallowed the Standard prescription for using language 'properly'.

Why not? One reason is that Standard English is not (as the Game **Talking 'Proper'?** (2.6) discusses) automatically, or exclusively, 'proper' English.

Speakers of English RP and users of Standard words and syntax cannot claim superiority for their language on the grounds of its archetypal purity. The English language has Germanic origins, and along the way has picked up traces of Celtic, Latin and Norman French.

Nor is Standard English more intricately or regularly structured than other versions of the language. Chomsky, the American linguist, has emphasized the structured, 'rule-based' nature of all languages. That is, all have regularly patterned syntax, so each can have a 'grammer' – a *description* – of this regular system of structure: in this sense, there are as many grammars as there are varieties.

Moreover, the various dialects of English all have the same functional potential, capable of generating the language of art or of everyday use with equal efficiency and aesthetic power (Shepherd 1990), whilst Standard English can be used intelligently or stupidly, rendered beautiful or ugly.

Even so, Kingman and subsequent curriculum directives have argued that the syntax and the lexicon of Standard English (though not an RP accent) should be taught first and foremost. Yet there is a fundamental difference between this new prescription and the old: Kingman does not suggest it should be swallowed without understanding the dosage or respecting and preserving its alternatives.

He acknowledges that every variety of English 'has its own authenticity' (Kingman 1988: 7): Non-standard varieties are 'a source of richness' of which speakers may be 'rightly proud' (1988: 14). However, Standard English has value as a language of national and world communication. Moreover, as Brian Cox (Chairman of the National Curriculum English Working Group given, in 1988, the brief of deciding programmes of study for all children from five to sixteen) notes:

> If pupils do not have access to Standard English then many important opportunities are closed to them, in cultural activities, in further and higher education, and in industry, commerce and the professions . . . In our democracy, Standard English confers power on its users, power to explain political issues and to persuade on a national and international stage.
>
> (Cox 1991: 29)

It is not that Non-standard varieties could not explain political issues, of course, rather that its discussion might be less respectfully listened to. Besides, because the Standard has traditionally commanded an authority not enjoyed by the Non-standard, it has, as Gillian Brown (1990: 35–6 and quoted in Cox) observes, accrued an 'astonishing wealth of vocabulary . . . through its intellectual and imperial history'. Therefore, in Kingman's view (1988: 14) and in Cox's (1991: 29), every child has a 'right' to acquire the Standard.

Nevertheless, Standard English is to be *added* to repertoires rather than forced as a replacement, the pragmatism of its choice, and its relationship to other varieties, to be understood and reflected upon.

Teaching to this new prescription is a tall order – far more difficult than adhering to the old, simple Standard, more challenging than merely immersing students in a generalized language awareness. And it will take time for understanding of what language really is, in all its complexity and creativity, its diversity and potency, to overcome old and ill-considered prejudices, particularly since these are frequently the consequences – as interdisciplinary linguistics, and some of the Games, demonstrate – of factors of life beyond language itself.

Ferdinand de Saussure, the Swiss linguist, made a brilliantly revealing comparison between the game of chess (its elements, rules and development) and language. But the analogy can be extended: chess can have only one winner and there must be a loser. *Playing the Language Game* may cause students to wonder how far this need be true in the real language world. Whatever players conclude, their chances of success must be increased by their experience of explicit learning about language and its place in human life.

The Games, with their experiential approach to the acquisition of critical linguistic knowledge and skills – in relation to a variety of human contexts and pressures – are thus one way of helping children to have their effective say, individually and collectively, in school and in their adult lives.

2 Playing the game

The Games in this book were originally designed to overcome a difficulty we were encountering with undergraduates. When 'linguistics' was mentioned to new students reading for Communications Studies or Humanities or Education degrees, their anxiety was almost palpable. They expected an abstract course, divorced from the language they actually used, and primarily based on the grammar which – given the recent rejections of language analysis discussed in Chapter 1 – was to many a daunting mystery. We wanted to overcome the nervousness that was a barrier to teaching and to relate theory to practice in a stimulating and challenging way.

Our experiments at The Nottingham Trent University, funded by the Enterprise Scheme, were encouraging, and it seemed they might be extended to younger students. So trials followed in schools and colleges in Leicestershire and Derbyshire. These included Charles Keene College of Further Education, Leicester; King Edward VII Community College, Coalville; and Tupton Hall School, Old Tupton, Chesterfield (pupils aged 11–18). Postgraduate trainee English teachers, in the Department of Education at Loughborough University, also gave me their opinions. I am extremely grateful to staff and students for playing the Games and for their constructive criticisms and suggestions. Their comments have been included in Chapter 3, at the end of each Game.

The Games

Purposes

The Games are generally experiential, inviting students (especially in Chapter 3, Section 2) to take part in, or to witness, language behaviour. Each is intended to stimulate the description, analysis and critical explanation (the basic features of language work discussed in Chapter 1) of that experience. They are not, unlike many other games, particularly simulation games, problem-solving exercises. And they are not designed to practise, and in this direct way to improve, language skills. Rather, they are intended to facilitate students' use of language, in the real world, by increasing their knowledge and understanding of language behaviour and also by bringing to their attention those attitudes (their own and those of others) which can be as powerful as language itself.

For example, **Talking Power** (2.3) takes as its starting point the widespread belief that men use language differently – and more powerfully – than women. But the Game does not automatically endorse this premise by encouraging female players to identify and to practise particularly powerful language strategies which they can then put to good use outside the classroom: it is not an exercise in assertiveness training. Instead, it puts male and female players together – without a pre-written script – in a situation conventionally involving power and control and observes what happens. The experience, for these players and those watching, is not precisely predictable but usually surprises the participants. In consequence, it stimulates the players' independent thinking on the matter and it is likely that this considered assessment will have more effect on their subsequent language behaviour than the mere parroting of conversational 'power' tactics might have generated. It certainly had a salutary influence on one, hitherto dominating, member of our group who, amazed to find himself playing 'weak' talk when cast in a powerless role, came to the conclusion that future seminars would be more productive if talking-power were distributed rather more evenly round the class and – having participated in the Game – had ideas on how to facilitate such a change. Knowledge and understanding had been gained – not only about language behaviour itself, but, equally importantly, the student had been brought face to face with, and to question, some of his previously unacknowledged attitudes to language performance.

It will be clear from this single example that the terms 'game' and 'player' are being used very loosely. I am aware of objections to such imprecision. Ken Jones (1987: 13), for example, points out that 'player' can imply self-conscious acting – not the immersion in unscripted experience which is intended for **Talking Power** (2.3) and for some of its companions. Moreover, gaming usually involves 'winning' and 'losing' but, as Taylor and Walford (1978: 31) point out, the aim of this kind of educational approach is not 'to produce self-satisfied winners in the way that a casual Monopoly session might do': success or failure would be inappropriate outcomes for activities that focus on observing process rather than achieving product. (On the other hand, some of the Games have power as one of their key issues and therefore must include, for someone, the experience of success – but simulated success, that is, in simulated life, not prowess as a competitive games player.)

However, 'game' is still a useful term for our purposes, since it is used here, firstly, to distinguish the practices we suggest from the more traditional kind of language exercise, generally done individually and privately, involving reading, writing, pen and paper – and getting that exercise right (or wrong). The activities we call games are varied, including some role-plays, some 'experiments', some collaborative investigations. Secondly, these activities are rightly called 'games' in the sense that none of them are quite real – and thus the language they involve is just sufficiently distanced from the language we take for granted, day in day out, so that players can be conscious of its features. Thirdly, like any game, these should always be interesting, often fun. But, most importantly, they are never – unlike Monopoly, or Snakes and Ladders – an end in themselves: they are merely beginnings, experiences of language behaviour and of language attitudes which, after the play is concluded are, with the help of staff, to be described and discussed in a critical context.

Themes

Each Game, with its critical follow-up, is complete in itself, to be accomplished in one class session. Some have Sequels and at the beginning of each Game there is cross-referencing to others on related issues. So selected Games may be played from time to time. Or as, in their given sequence, there is a logical progression from the theme of one to the focus of the next, a number could be played in successive weeks.

That logical progression is not based on the child's development (indeed, it should be noted that several of the Games may be adapted for play at a variety of ages) but is, instead, thematic. It relates, roughly, to the 'model' described in the Report of the Committee of Inquiry into the Teaching of English Language, chaired by Sir John Kingman (1988: 17–31). This model details in four parts those features of language (particularly English language), and its usage, which the Committee believes children should be helped to explicitly understand. The model includes (1988: 17):

- Part 1: The forms of the English language – sounds, letters, works, sentences, and how these relate to meaning
- Part 2: Communication and comprehension – how speakers and writers communicate and how listeners and readers understand them
- Part 3: Acquisition and development – how the child acquires and develops language
- Part 4: Historical and geographical variation – how language changes over time, and how languages which are spread over territories differentiate into dialects or indeed into separate languages.

The Games in Chapter 3, Section 1 of this volume relate principally to Part 1 of the Kingman model, because they deal with aspects of the meaningful language resources (words, sentences, sounds), available to each user. For instance, **Signing** (1.1) and its Sequels demonstrate, through Games involving sketching and miming, the differences between the words of symbolic language and other kinds of sign. It also relates to the equally expressive language of those whose hearing is impaired. **We're Only Human** (1.2) plays with a crucial difference between animal and human communication – the meaningful placing of symbolic language in complex structures. Its Sequel, with the help of e.e. cummings's poetry, invites students to experiment with their own structural creativity. References to structure, however, raise the spectre of the much-feared grammar, so **Knowing the Rules** (1.3) aims to dispel this anxiety by asking students to draw what they see in a nonsense poem, convincing them that in a very real sense they already know all there is to know about the rules of syntax. There is also an opportunity here, for older students, to think about language acquisition, especially in relation to Chomsky's identification of our language knowledge as 'competence'. **Identikits** (1.4) puts language knowledge into practice, through everyday language and the language of literature. Next, **Jigsaw Puzzles** (1.5) deals with some of the 'rules' of our knowledge and demonstrates that a rule-based competence is in no sense confining but is essential to our creativity. Its Sequel looks at the morphological and syllabic play of the feminist movement and also of Rastafarian language. **Sounds Suspicious** (1.6) then turns from words and structures to the sounds from which they are made. It requires players to imagine they are detectives solving a crime through the use of phonetic description. **Sound Sense** (1.7) plays with just two words and makes these mean various things through shifts of intonation and rhythm. Finally, in Section 1, **Language for Living** (1.8) asks players to tell stories through usual and unusual metaphors, questioning the degree to which choices from our available language resources construct our realities. Its Sequel invites older students to look at the extent to which metaphor may shape our reaction to AIDS.

Knowing the Rules (1.3) also links, through its discussion of language acquisition, with some of Part 3 of the Kingman model.

The Games in Chapter 3, Section 2 relate roughly to Parts 2 and 4 of the Kingman model, focusing on our *use* – in different cultural and social contexts – of the signs and structures that are our language resources. These Games also deal with attitudes to that use. For example, **Variety Performance** (2.1) and its Sequel, **What's my line?**, play with choices from our language resources in relation to the people and purposes involved in a situation. **Sounds Familiar** (2.2) plays with dialects and advertising, raising issues about attitudes to Non-standard English. **Talking 'Proper'?** (2.6) stages a debate on similar issues. **Laying Down the Language Law** (2.9) extends the debate into imaginary overseas government committees. **Talking Power** (2.3) wonders whether women are inevitably disadvantaged linguistically or whether power differentials, affecting both men and women, are the root of language inequality. **Cross Talk** (2.4) compares language use cross-culturally. **Cracking the Joke!** (2.5) and its Sequel, **Winning words**, play with TV comedy scripts – and real-life tragedy – in order to allow students to identify language manipulation. **Form and Focus** (2.8) and also **Shaping Thought** (2.7) look at the linguistic manipulation of perception. (The Games in Section 2 are divided into two groups. The first group, Games 2.1–2.5, are concerned principally with spoken language; the second group, Games 2.6–2.9, relate to either spoken or written language.)

Methods of play

On the whole, the Games are designed for students aged 13–18, but most can be adapted for younger players (some suggestions are made to this end) and all can be useful for students in further and higher education as well at school.

About 25 players is a comfortable maximum, but more can be accommodated and many of the Games will need to be played in smaller sub-groups (operating simultaneously). A spacious room is needed for several of the Games – preferably, for some of them, sound-proofed!

Staff participation in a Game is rarely called for: indeed, since the players' behaviour must be as spontaneous and student-centred as possible for it to be a useful experience, directing a Game's outcomes should be avoided. Teachers are, in effect, simply producers of the play, helping to set the process in motion and to keep it going. And none of the Games, with the exception of **Sounds Suspicious** (1.6) – probably the most difficult Game to play in many respects – require much in the way of props or preparation other than, on occasion, some photocopying before the class.

Teachers are also referees, ready to see fair play. Usually this is not a problem. The Games are generally non-threatening, safely contained within the classroom context. Even so, language use is behaviour, and because it is behaviour which in some sense expresses/represents identity, then playing games with it could create – even more than is a potential hazard in any discipline's games – counter-productive tensions and embarrassments. For instance, role playing any class-related or race-related game could be sensitive in some mixed groups, and the time and opportunity needed to resolve any problems that could arise might not be available. So the Games avoid some areas, or only touch on them in distanced ways. **Sounds Familiar** (2.2) and **Talking 'Proper'?** (2.6), for example, do have a social class reference, but the former uses adverts as its focus, and the latter is structured as a debate *about* issues. Thus, players are not required, in either case, to demonstrate or to discuss directly their own, personal, variety of English (unless they so choose).

More generally, again because language is so closely linked to identity, role playing can be threatening even without touching on particularly sensitive themes. Teachers might therefore choose to avoid some Games when a group contains specially difficult personality mixes.

On the other hand, since the Games encourage group cooperation, they may, paradoxically, help overcome these very difficulties. And some, **Signing** (1.1) or **Variety Performance** (2.1), are specially designed as ice-breakers, introductions not simply to language but to group work and to games playing itself. Obviously, the Games work better the more relaxed their participants have become. Not only will players be able to think more clearly but, also, the more comfortable the participants, the more likely their language behaviour is to resemble the genuine and spontaneous.

And, of course, it is participation in behaviour that resembles in some way genuine language use, in the real world, that is crucial to the majority of the Games. Some older students have, at first, believed that an explanation of the issues involved, in chalk and talk form, would give them information about language – all they feel they need. But, having once played language games, they generally come to believe that *experiencing* causes them to take note of, to remember – and be intrigued by – aspects of language in all their intricacies of system and practice. This is, apparently, not because Games are just an entertaining change from chalk, talk and write, but because participants *feel* what happens as they play, and thus become aware of the effect that language has upon themselves and others.

These reactions are the necessary precondition for the vital 'debriefing' that follows all the Games. For although each Game can be played in a very few minutes, far more time will be needed for the analysis and critical explanation that is so crucial to this experiential approach.

For instance, the improvised mini-drama of **Talking Power** (2.3) can be staged in 10 minutes. But its implications will take some time to pinpoint and assess. At this stage, teachers change their role from producer to prompt, ready in the wings to encourage the post-Game discussion, to provide it with helpful metalanguage and, most importantly, the pegs on which the discussion may be hung.

These pegs – an explanation of the element of the language resources, or the language function, played with in the Game – are explained in detail in each 'Point of the Game' (assuming, for the non-specialist, no previous linguistic expertise). Related further reading is mentioned, but a Game's essentials are included in its 'Point'.

Occasionally, teachers may find it convenient to outline this 'Point' before the play, but generally, except in the case of **Talking Proper?** (2.6), this need not be done until after issues have been raised by the Game itself. In any case, few of the Games – language being as complex and creative as it is – have highly predictable outcomes and the emphasis of the discussion will thus vary from class to class. Besides, as already mentioned, it is preferable not to pre-empt the play, otherwise the 'genuineness' of the experience may be lost. This can be particularly important when attitudes are the subject of a Game [as in **Sounds Familiar** (2.2)]: these are likely to be more authentic and to show up more clearly and convincingly if they are encountered without warning [though, as just suggested, **Talking Proper?** (2.6) is a rather different case].

Discussion usually goes well. Everyone has something to talk about because everyone has witnessed or taken part in the Game – and if the Point has not been established beforehand, there can be no fear of saying something stupid through having forgotten what the textbook, or the teacher, said.

But the discussion will not be imprecise or aimless. For even when only a small number of the students have actually experienced language behaviour in a Game (as they took part in, say, a mini-drama) no one has been passive. The rest of the class have, on these occasions, been involved in the play as linguists, observing as if they were researchers in the field. In consequence, everyone should be ready for the careful description and analysis – the basic essentials of language work described in Chapter 1 – of their observations. And, given these basics, discussion and explanation of language behaviour can be much more than superficial, unfounded chat.

In this way, linguistic skills, as well as knowledge about language and aware-ness of attitudes to language, are also being developed as the Games are played. These skills can be utilized again by following the Games with project work.

Follow-up: Project work

The Games and their debriefing, considering their 'Points', need not be the end of classroom work. Because of the interest they encourage, the insights they stimulate, and because of the skills of linguistic observation, description, analysis and explanation that they practise, Games can be a helpful preparation for language project work. Suggestions for this are made in Chapter 4.

Project work is an effective bridge between the classroom experience of language and its spontaneous use outside the school gate. For it carries aca-demic investigation beyond simulated contexts into the families, and into the social and work places that students encounter in their lives out of school, encouraging them to hear the language of these with an informed and critical ear.

Projects therefore finish the job the Games begin, demonstrating the vital importance, and relevance, of learning about the language that people really read, write and speak.

3 The Games

The 'rules' (of language)

We all know the rules and conventions of using language, because:

(a) We have developed what the American linguist, Noam Chomsky, has called *competence*: that is, knowledge – more or less unconscious – about the 'rules' of our language, the ways in which the sounds, words and combinations of words can be formed and grouped meaningfully together.

Imagine a box of children's Lego bricks. There is a finite number of different coloured bricks in the set together with a sheet of instructions explaining that they can be combined by fitting them together, the top of one slotting into the bottom of another. With these limited materials, used according to this single rule, the Lego player can make any number of models, creating buildings and objects and creatures, some of which have been seen before and some that are invented entirely fresh out of the builder's imagination.

The same is true of language. Each language has a finite set of materials: sounds (or, in the case of language used by those with hearing impairment, signs made with the body). Each has a set of rules. And each, with its limited number of different sounds or signs, arranged together into words and groups of words according to its particular rules, gives its users the means to say, in theory, anything they want to in that particular language.

Clearly, unlike rules of the law, say, or even of etiquette, these rules need not be restrictive. On the contrary, far from being a repressive hindrance, they are the key to our language expertise.

They are rules known to its users whether or not they have ever had a formal grammar lesson. Its speakers acquired them in childhood, without any deliberate teaching.

They were acquired more or less unconsciously. But, given the *explicit* understanding recommended by the Kingman Report (1988), discussed in Chapter 1, these rules may be used even more effectively, heard more clearly.

They are the main subject of Section 1 of the Games. This Section roughly matches (as explained in Chapter 1) Parts 1 and 3 of the Kingman model of English.

(b) We also acquired, as we grew up, a different sort of rule – or perhaps set of conventions, or defining patterns, would be a better way of putting it. That is, we have all acquired what has been called *communicative competence* (Hymes 1971) – we have learned how to put the words and grammatical structures we know into use.

Sometimes we were taught this usage directly: 'remember to say "please" and "thank you"'. Sometimes we have absorbed conventions from the language behaviour going on around us. So we know, for example, what conversation is usually like in our particular culture – and we know that when language behaviour does not follow the fundamental rule or convention of our culture, sharing the talk in some proportion between participants, that we are listening not to a conversation but to a monologue. Different cultures have different 'rules' of communicative competence. Some Chilean Indians, for instance, do not expect women to join in the conversations which emphasize, for them, masculinity: the wife sits silently facing the wall!

So, the first set of rules (a) gives all human beings the 'competence' to be infinitely, individually, creative – in theory. I say 'in theory' because the second set of conventions (b) (some of which are examined in Section 2 of the Games, the topics of which roughly match those of Parts 2 and 4 of the Kingman model), though its strictures can be flouted, limits the linguistic options open to us.

The Games and activities that follow, particularly in Section 2, illustrate, and invite players to consider and to question, this fundamental tension.

Moreover, if we accept communicative competence's related concept of 'appropriacy' – the assumption that we learn to use language in the butcher's shop, the doctor's surgery, to friends, to parents, and so on, in different and typical ways that are *appropriate* and *normal* to the people and situation involved – how do we view the language of those who do not follow these conventions? For to disregard such language habits may be to challenge accepted patterns of social behaviour and power relations. Is this always, by definition, *in*appropriate and *ab*normal? Or is it sometimes [as 'critical' linguists, including for example Norman Fairclough (1989) in his discussions of language use and inequality, might argue], an example of creative competence?

The rules (of the Games)

The Games have one general rule [with a significant exception in the case of **Talking 'Proper'?** (2.6)]: that is, play first, talk after. As explained in Chapter 2, it is important to take this approach in order for players to be able to talk helpfully about their *experience* of language.

Each Game, its 'Play' and its 'Point', is therefore explained in the following way.

1 First, there is a very brief description of the Game's focus, followed by the suggested age range, the likely preparation time involved, and a list of other Games dealing with related issues.
2 Then the Game itself is described.
3 The 'Point' of the Game comes next. Specialist staff will obviously be conversant with the Point before playing, and non-specialists will read it in conjunction with the Game. The Point does not precede the Game, however, because it will not become clear to student players until *after* the Game has been experienced. My discussion therefore takes its cue from the Game itself and refers back to issues that will arise through the play.
4 If the Game has 'Sequels', these come next, because they are usually played in the light of the Point – the explicit knowledge which may be acquired through the basic Game and its follow-up discussion.
5 Finally, there is an 'Afterword'. This includes observations about the practicalities or the usefulness of play, made by staff and students from Tupton Hall School, Chesterfield; King Edward VII Community College, Coalville; Charles Keene College of Further Education, Leicester; Loughborough University Department of Education (PGCE); and The Nottingham Trent University Department of English and Media Studies – all of whom have experimented with the Games.

SECTION 1
THE ELEMENTS OF LANGUAGE

1.1 SIGNING

Sequels: **Visual signs, No comment, Signing without sound**

Focus: The arbitrary symbolic nature of language signs compared to iconic and indexical signs. The Sequel **No comment** links these matters to intonation and stress [a topic developed in **Sound Sense** 1.7] and **Signing without sound** relates them to sign language used by those with a hearing impairment. There is also a brief Sequel entitled **Visual signs**.

Age range: Top Juniors to Higher Education.

Preparation time: Nil.

Related Games: **We're Only Human** (1.2), **Knowing the Rules** (1.3), **Jigsaw Puzzles** (1.5), **Sound Sense** (1.7).

The Game

The group should divide into pairs. First, each person in each pair should draw four items that have been important to him or her in recent weeks. At least one of these 'items' should relate to some important event, place, person or object. At least one other should relate to an idea, or to a feeling. While the drawing is taking place, there should be no talking. When the sketches are complete, they should be exchanged – still without conversation – between partners. Now each student should try to deduce – again without talk – what he or she can about the meaning of the four drawings he or she has been given. When the students have worked out as much as they can on their own, the pairs may begin to talk about the implications of their sketches. The artists can now explain what they had actually intended their pictures to signify, filling in gaps in their partner's understanding. Finally, each pair should discuss their guesses – and how far they matched the artist's intentions – with the group as a whole.

The Point of the Game

(a) It should help to break the games-playing ice.
(b) It draws attention to, defines, and raises issues about, the comparative communicative power of different kinds of signs: *icons*, *indexes* and, by contrast, the *arbitrary symbols* of language [terms originally employed by the philosopher and logician, C.S. Pierce (see Fiske 1982: 49–52)]. Arbitrary symbols contribute to the tremendous linguistic creativity which is arguably a defining feature of our very 'humanness' [a concept which is developed, with particular reference to the 'structures' into which language symbols fit, in **We're Only Human** (1.2)].

If, for example, the artist wants to signal the importance of a particular place to his or her partner, then he or she could draw that place as clearly as possible: in so doing, the artist would produce an 'iconic' sign, closely resembling the location. If, on the other hand, he or she signalled this place by drawing one of its significant features, or something closely related to it – the Eiffel Tower perhaps, if the place in mind is Paris – then he or she has drawn an 'index' of the place, a pointer to it, for indexes (like smoke in relation to fire, spots in relation to measles) have an actual connection with their referent. (Of course, the drawing of a tower is also iconic, looking like the building. But it will be clear that it has not been drawn as an iconic sign if the artist rejects its interpretation as 'tower' but accepts an indexical answer.)

When the partners start to talk (or write) about the drawings, however, then they are using a different sort of signing: *symbolic* language. It is symbolic in the sense that the words for the location – 'foreign capital', maybe, or 'tourist city' – are *arbitrary*. That is, they do not look, or sound anything like (*iconically*), the place itself. Nor do they refer to it in any intrinsically (*indexically*) related way. They are, in their way, as arbitrary as the symbols of mathematics. A tree need not be a 'tree': it could be referred to as a 'zipzup' or a 'slogo' – and of course in French it is *arbre*, in German *baum*, and so on.

There are certain exceptions to this general principle of arbitrariness in language: *onomatopoeic* words, like 'quack', are iconic because they do bear resemblance to their referent. In English, these are relatively rare, though in some other languages – Korean and Japanese for instance – a substantial proportion of vocabulary is onomatopoeic. We also make some indexical sounds: the exclamation, 'ouch', is a sign directly connected with pain.

But of course language signs need not even be sounds. The sign for 'tree' could just as easily be one of the hand signals – many of them arbitrary – used by those with impaired hearing. (We shall return to this kind of sign below under **Signing without sound**.)

Our symbolic language system is, in a number of ways, including its arbitrariness, a bit like chess [an analogy drawn by the Swiss linguist, Ferdinand de Saussure (1857–1913)]. If we were shipwrecked on a desert island, and our chess set had gone down with our ship, we could still play the game. We could choose bits of driftwood or pebbles for the pieces. Anything would do, so long as these arbitrarily chosen items were distinctly different from each other and so long as we all *agreed* which item represented which piece in the game.

It is the same with words. For example, 'cat', 'hat' and 'rat' are all recognizably different (because each has a different first consonant) and we agree to recognize these different symbols as signifying three different things. That is, we agree, more or less, on the meanings of the words: the arbitrary symbols of human language have (unlike the vaguer grunts and growls of animals) relatively precise meanings or *semanticity*.

Now, to return to the drawings, it is very unlikely that the indexical sketches, or even the iconic ones – unless the group contains extremely skilled, trained artists – will convey sufficient information for the students to guess their creators' precise intentions in every case (though see the Sequel, **Visual signs**, below). The players will generally be unable to convey all they want to without the power of arbitrary, symbolic human language.

This power is communicative in conjunction with certain other defining features of language. These 'design features' were comprehensively listed and explained by Charles Hockett (his fullest list is in Hockett and Altmann 1968). They include – in addition to the arbitrariness and semanticity we have just mentioned – displacement, duality, structure dependence and cultural transmission. Displacement is particularly relevant to the Point of this Game and is discussed immediately below. Some of the other features are dealt with in **We're Only Human** (1.2) or **Knowing the Rules** (1.3).

As regards *displacement*, few other creatures apart from human beings appear to demonstrate this capacity. It allows its users to talk about something not present in the immediate context. We can say, 'Our Aunt Bertha, who emigrated to Australia in the fifties, is coming back to England next week.' That is, we can refer to a person who is not standing before us but who is living in a far distant place: we may never even have met her. We can talk about something she did many years ago. We can predict something in her future. We can even make all of this up! Aunt Bertha does not need to exist anywhere, any time, for us to refer to such a person: human beings can tell lies. For, because the speakers of a human language agree, more or less, on the meanings of their linguistic symbols, these symbols are significant even when, in the absence of the supporting, explanatory contexts to which they refer (like the subjects of the players' drawings), they are *displaced*.

Animals, on the other hand, do not appear to have displacement in their communicative capacity. On the whole, they can only, very generally, communicate their immediate responses to an immediate situation. So dogs can bark or growl their disapproval of a passing cat – as it passes. But they cannot, when we return from school or work, tell us how next door's cat came through the garden and annoyed them earlier in the day. This is partly because dogs apparently do not have any arbitrary symbol for 'cat' or for 'trespasser'. The sounds they make are indexical, linked to their experiences, more or less as they happen. Bees are a little different. They can return to their hives and report, through the language of a dance, the location of nectar some distance away. But their messages to fellow bees are confined to mapping the source of nectar and are still indexical because they are only made if the bees have actually been in contact with the nectar. They could not discuss this year's honey sales, or the state of next door's garden.

We are not so restricted in the topics of our conversations. Our range of symbols is potentially unlimited, in part because our ability to apply *morphological rules* [see **Jigsaw Puzzles** (1.5)] helps us to create fresh symbols for any eventuality. In sum, in association with other language design features, the symbolic signs of human language allow us, theoretically, to be infinitely creative and subtly meaningful.

Sequels

Visual signs

Although **Signing** (1.1) should illustrate the tremendous communicative power of symbolic language, some students may find that, in a few instances, their pictures convey meaning as efficiently – or even more so – than words. In this case, a discussion of visual signs may be generated. For instance, a student may have drawn a person holding out a single rose to another person. The picture, because of the rose's traditional associations in our culture, is likely to signify to the watching students an offering of love. The small drawing thus conveys, economically and powerfully, as much or more than several words. Visual signs are, however, outside the brief of this book and the interested player might like to follow the topic up in, for example, Fiske (1982).

No comment

It is possible to explore the issue of meaning and displacement further – if the class is well-established and if it contains at least one willing clown! At the same time, this Sequel draws attention to the vital part played, in the communication of meaning, by intonation and stressed sound. It could also, therefore, be played in connection with **Sound Sense** (1.7).

A 1990s television commercial for a French wine was wordless (apart from a brief, endorsing voice-over at the end). As the wine was poured and drunk, viewers just heard grunts, of varying tones and stress, which seemed to be indexes of varying kinds and degrees of appreciation. One of the students should try something similar. He or she should privately choose a product and then advertise it (perhaps, in the process, making disparaging reference to a similar but in her view 'inferior' product) with those qualities of voice which – like, for example, breathy, gravelly, husky or whiney tones – are called *paralinguistic* features. The student should sound these with varying intonation and rhythm. That is, like the television actors, he or she should perform without words – *but, unlike the TV actors, he or she should do so also without scenery or props and without body gestures.* Given these restrictions, it is not likely that the group will be able to guess the chosen product, what it is and what it is for.

But the listening students will probably know, from the sound patterns, whether they are hearing references to the approved or to the *dis*approved product. And in this way the actor will have demonstrated that intonation, stress and paralinguistic tones, the kinds of sounds he or she has been permitted to use, do have meaning. They can convey, among other things, our emotional responses and can emphasize what is important to us. If the actor is particularly skilful, she may even be able to suggest a certain kind of approval (relish, joy, comfort, and so on) or disapproval (distaste, perhaps, or disdain).

Stress and intonation (and the paralinguistic) are thus vital to communication, and the Game [in conjunction with **Sound Sense** (1.7) perhaps] may encourage students to use such signals more clearly and effectively. But on their own, as the watchers' inability to guess the products should prove, they are limited. In this way, the actor's limitations should, indirectly, reinforce the student's understanding of the comparatively restricted signalling power of animal cries. Dogs bark, cats mew, horses neigh very generalized messages. But on the whole, animals – like the actor in this Game – do not appear to 'say' anything very specific.

However, the television advert is not so restricted as the student actor who is allowed no scenery and no props. In the commercial, viewers see the product itself and the relevant context and referents of the sounds: that is, there is no question of *displacement*. The vision of a beautiful sunny day, the actors standing on a patio with wine bottle and glasses, drawing the cork and then sipping their wine with obvious pleasure, gave an enormous amount of information in conjunction with the feelings conveyed by the TV actors' wordless sounds.

Students playing this Game, on the other hand, have to try to 'talk' about something that is not present in the room. That is, they must try to cope with displacement – but without the benefit of arbitrary symbolic language. Because they are virtually doomed to failure, the Game should reinforce the students' understanding of the human capacity for displacement, helped by arbitrary symbolic language.

Signing without sound

(I am indebted to Lindsay Davies, a student in Nottingham Polytechnic's Department of English and Media Studies, for background to the following discussion.)

Students could take their discussion of symbol/icon/index on to a consideration of the silent signing used by those with impaired hearing. They might consider the powerful communicative mixture of symbolic, iconic and indexical signing in, for example, British Sign Language.

Cued Speech and Finger Spelling are, in some sense, 'translations' of spoken language. The hand signs of Cued Speech stand for, and thus draw attention to, the sounds of speech, as they occur, so that those watching can use them to assist lip-reading. Finger Spelling has signs which refer to the written alphabet. British Sign Language (BSL), however, in a similar way to American Sign Language (ASL), works on different principles.

On the whole, its signs are not iconic or indexical: they do not often look like, or link in some obvious way to, their referent. But, as in spoken English, there are exceptions. 'Gardening' is signalled by a kind of scooping motion – something like a trowel digging.

The vast majority of signs, though, are arbitrarily symbolic. One sign involves the tips of the fingers bunching together. The bunch made by one hand touches the bunch made by the other and then the hands, fingertips still together, move apart with a wiggling motion. This is a signal for linguistics!

The sign for 'brown' may be made by a hand stroking the forearm. Perhaps this had indexical origins in a brown, suntanned arm. But, in another part of England, the colour is signalled by the straightened fingers of one hand moving rapidly up and down. It is difficult to see any indexical link here, and certainly no iconic one.

Since signs, like 'brown', do alter regionally (just as, for instance, spoken English may call a passage-way between houses an 'alley' in one part of the country, a 'ginnel' elsewhere), and as they may also differ according to other variables like age, there are evidently dialects of BSL. The 'accent' of BSL may vary too. That is, words may remain basically the same but they are marginally different in different areas – just as the same spoken words can be pronounced slightly differently, Scouse sounding different from Cockney, and both being different from Geordie. So, 'man', in one part of the country, is signalled by pulling at the chin. In another district, the sign looks a bit more like a beard being tugged.

Where spoken language uses intonation and stress for the expression of degree or emphasis, signs of the BSL kind may be repeated.

Repetition has other uses too. It may indicate notions like plurality and, also, the aspect (e.g. duration, continuity, completion) of the verb.

Unlike ordinary spoken/written language, BSL is spatial. That is, whilst spoken language is delivered serially, word following word in time, sign language takes place in the space around the body. One consequence of this difference is that signs can be simultaneously meaningful. Sometimes this is an advance over spoken language. For where in spoken language we may say 'The bus passed under the bridge' – mentioning first the bus and then the bridge – we could make a sign for a bridge and, more or less at the same time, beneath it, make a sign for a bus.

Space is also used by BSL to indicate tense, through a kind of iconic metaphor appropriate to our culture's sense of time. That is, signs which take place quite near to the body refer to the present. Those slightly back from these signal the past. Those made at a small distance in front of the body refer to the future – appropriately enough, since in our culture we tend to imagine what has yet to happen as being ahead of ourselves.

Like the language of sound, then, this kind of sign language can be said to be rule-governed, working according to regularly observed principles. However, rule government is not the subject of **Signing** (1.1) and its Sequels [it is discussed in other Games including **We're Only Human** (1.2) and **Knowing the Rules** (1.3)] and the reader who wishes to follow the point up in relation to language used by the deaf could do so in, for example, Klima and Bellugi (1979), Deucher (1984) and Miles (1988).

Finally, facial expressions and body movements are, as in spoken language, indicative of meaning in addition to silent signs themselves.

Afterword

Game plan

(a) Initially, I gave players less time to do the drawings of **Signing** (1.1) than to discuss them afterwards. But it turned out that longer was required for the sketching, particularly when this was the first game the students had played and when, consequently, a touch of anxiety was slowing them down.

(b) It is essential to make clear that the drawings will be given to someone else for comment – otherwise they may become mere squiggles, of no possible significance except to their creators.

(c) It is advisable to write on the board (using symbolic language!) suggestions for two kinds of drawings – 'objects' in one list, abstracts in the other – and insist that at least one picture per person is of the abstract kind. Otherwise, most of the drawings may be icons of 'concrete' items and therefore not too difficult to place.

Tutor and student comment

(a) When played with new, first-year polytechnic students, I thought the silence of drawing time might be threatening for a class which was meeting for the first time. Afterwards, the students assured me this was not the case. On the contrary, they were only just getting into the swing of seminar work and those who were finding it difficult to talk 'on demand', as it were, welcomed a chance to accomplish a task quietly and privately (something of an irony for a language class!).

(b) Warning! After the initial silence during the drawing period, the game becomes very noisy when sketches are exchanged for discussion.

1.2 WE'RE ONLY HUMAN

Sequel: **Poetry and patterning**

Focus: The 'humanness' of language, particularly its syntactic structure dependence (with brief reference to Chomsky), but also explaining, in the Point of the Game, other significant features of human communication [including arbitrariness, duality, semanticity, displacement and cultural transmission, some of which are discussed in **Signing** (1.1)]. **We're Only Human** (1.2) plays with everyday language; its Sequel, **Poetry and patterning**, works with poetry.

Age range: The first half of the basic Game (1.2a) could be played with relatively young children using simple sentences. However, the rest of this Game (1.2b and 1.2c) and its Point are more suitable for older students (aged approximately 14 plus). Its Sequel contains two activities related to the creative uses of language.

Preparation time: Some photocopying of sentences and poems could be helpful, otherwise nil.

Related Games: **Signing** (1.1), **Knowing the Rules** (1.3), **Identikits** (1.4), **Jigsaw Puzzles** (1.5).

The Game

(a) Players, working individually or in small groups, should rearrange the words of the sentences that follow in as many different, but meaningful, ways as possible. Relatively straightforward sentences might be used with younger children. For instance:

    1 The hippo on the television was sitting eating his breakfast.

    2 His name was Harry.

The children might rearrange these sentences to form

    3 The hippo was sitting on the television eating his breakfast.

    4 Was his name Harry?

The sentences could, of course, be printed on card and cut, word by word, into a jigsaw puzzle for experimental rearrangement.

  Older students could do more interesting rearrangements with a complex sentence like the following:

    5 Unhappily the man to the left of the government was arguing vainly
      for her.

For instance, they might suggest:

    6 Was the man to the left of the government, unhappily, arguing
      vainly for her?

Or – producing total changes of meaning – students might suggest:

    7 Unhappily for her, the man was arguing vainly to the left of the
      government.

or

    8 To her, unhappily for the man, the left of the government was
      arguing vainly.

But they would not, for example, suggest:

    9 Unhappily the man to left of the government was arguing vainly
      for her.

Why not?

(b) When all the alternatives are exhausted, students might try taking one of
    their sentences and replacing its words with other syntactically – and
    semantically – suitable ones, i.e. words which will not alter the original
    structure of the sentence and will still make some kind of sense. For
    instance:

    10 The hippo on the television was sitting *gobbling* a cheeseburger.

The original 'eating' could even be replaced by a verb which is not directly linked to food but is still relatively meaningful (if hippos could only hold a pencil!). For example:

    11 The hippo on the television was sitting *drawing* a cheeseburger.

As for the alternative sentence, alterations might be made like the following.

    12 ... the man was *shouting* vainly ...

(c) Finally, wherever possible, players might try substituting single words for whole phrases in any of their sentences. Instead of 'The hippo was sitting on the television eating a cheeseburger', they might suggest:

13 *He* was sitting *there* eating *it*.

Instead of 'Unhappily the man was arguing vainly for her', they might suggest:

14 Unhappily *he* was arguing vainly for her.

The Point of the Game

All of us, as we discuss in **Knowing the Rules** (1.3), appear to be in some way innately predisposed to language. And the defining features of this human form of communication have not been discovered – in entirety, at least – in any other creature. Language thus seems to be a crucial element of 'humanness' (see Aitchison, 1989, from which much of the following discussion derives, for a development of the matters touched on below).

Some of the characteristics, or *design features*, of human language [mentioned in **Signing** (1.1)] are also found to occur *naturally* in other creatures. Alternatively, chimpanzees have been *taught* to use symbols to communicate – up to a point. But only human beings seem naturally to understand and depend to a significant extent upon patterned *structuring* in their communication. *Structure dependence* therefore appears to be a crucially defining characteristic of 'humanness'.

Moreover, this characteristic – far from being an inhibiting sort of dependence – is an aspect of language that is vital to our theoretically infinite linguistic creativity (the central Point of this Game's Sequel).

To begin with, *duality* – a kind of structuring – is a potent feature of human language. We have a finite number of sounds but, because we are not restricted to using these individually, their potential is far from finite. We can put them together in order to make a limitless number of words. In this sense, language is a two-tier operation.

For example, the three sounds 't', 'o', 'p' – meaningless on their own in English – can be put together in three different ways to make *top*, *pot* and *opt*. The procedure is creative, a bit like play with Lego bricks in which a small number can be put together to form any number of models. But there are restrictions on the ways in which these particular sounds can be fixed together. For instance, we could not, in English, begin a word with the structure 'tpo'. Our dual system follows agreed, subconsciously known patterns (and other languages follow other patterns). Most other creatures do not appear to possess duality, but bird song seems to have it to a degree: single notes are meaningless, yet they apparently convey messages when strung together.

A further important, structural source of creativity is *slot filling*, the sort of manoeuvre tried in stage (b) of this Game. Words from a wide range that are syntactically and semantically suitable [and see **Identikits** (1.4) for semantically 'odd' fillers] can fill 'slots' in a sentence. Some chimpanzees have been able to manage simple operations of this kind. One called Sarah was taught to manipulate plastic tokens, each one signifying a word [chimps cannot make human sounds but, of course, as we saw in **Signing** (1.1), a human communication system does not have to use sound in order to be effective as language]. For instances, she would choose from a number of symbols for different colours, slotting her chosen symbol into the appropriate place: a *green* dish, a *yellow* dish or a *red* dish.

But Sarah stuck to a given word order. Yet, as this Game demonstrates [in sentences (1–9)], our understanding of the possible word orders of our particular language is very significant and contributes vastly to our creativity. Change the order of words in a sentence and their significance can change: 'the bus hit the child' means something very different from 'the child hit the bus'. No other creature appears able to create meaning from this manipulation of language structures. Washoe, one of the most famous apes involved in language experiments, was taught a version of American Sign Language. She acquired at least 100 signs, including one for 'sweet', which she used to refer to raspberry bushes, and one for 'go'. But sometimes Washoe would sign 'Go sweet' – and sometimes she would sign 'Sweet go'. If children used the latter word order, it is unlikely that they would be taken to find raspberries or any other sort of treat: it would probably be concluded that they meant the treat itself had somehow 'gone'. Washoe's carers, however, interpreted either word order to mean a desire for raspberries and so in either case took her to find the fruit. Perhaps, given time, she would eventually have settled down to a normal human (English, in this case) word order, but she grew so big and potentially dangerous that the experiment could not continue.

Children, however, take very little time to acquire the structuring rules of their particular language. So, even if chimps *could*, ultimately, be taught a kind of language system that resembles our own, it does not seem that they are naturally predisposed to it in the way that human beings evidently are.

For human beings know, apparently without deliberate teaching [see **Knowing the Rules** (1.3)], that whole chunks of utterances are structures that 'belong' together and so must be dealt with together. In consequence, students will not consider separating the words in (2) above which make up the phrase 'His name': The whole phrase can be moved, turning example (2) into (4), but it must remain intact. It is as though we recognize an invisible structure, linking parts of a sentence.

In fact, the American linguist, Noam Chomsky, has argued that we could describe our knowledge of sentence structures by saying that they have two layers, a *deep structure* and a *surface structure* (see Lyons 1991). The following sentences (the last of them a well-known example) seem to confirm our knowledge of something of the sort.

(x) Fighter planes can be dangerous.

(y) War planes can be dangerous.

(z) Flying planes can be dangerous.

In each sentence, a different word slots in before 'planes', describing them. In (x) and (y), it would seem we have chosen from a list of possible adjectives to pinpoint the exact planes that can be a danger to us. But (z) is different: there is ambiguity here. Does the sentence mean that planes can be dangerous if you get in their way when they are flying? Or does it mean that people who fly planes are in danger through their act of flying? If we decide it means the first alternative, then we are assuming the phrase 'flying planes' implies a particular syntactic structure [(x) and (y) are based on the same one] with 'planes' as its subject. If we decide on the second alternative, however, then it is as if we are assuming the phrase has a 'deep structure' in which 'people', or some such notion, are subject. If students drew a picture representing the first notion, they would somehow emphasize the planes themselves, whereas if they sketched the second, they would show anxious pilots: the subject of their images would be different to match the different grammatical subject of the sentence they are representing.

Our knowledge of sentences is evidently very complex. It is not restricted to simple slot filling. However, Chomsky's deep/surface structure model, though it clearly helps to explain what we know about the meaningful structures of sentences, may not explain how we put them together in the first place or how, as we listen to them, we understand them. (Chomsky does not claim that it does and, in any case, his arguments have developed over the last 40 years: see Aitchison 1987.) The whole question is much more complicated than we have space to discuss here. We can only highlight the Point that structure exists in human language, it matters to meaning, and we know it matters. Aitchison (1989) is essential reading for anyone needing to read around, and beyond, this basic starting point. Lyons (1991) focuses on Chomsky.

However, I want to stay for a moment with the way in which language structure seems to fall into units and the way in which we are able to replace these chunks *en bloc* with substitute language. This happened not only in the case of the planes but also in stage (c) of the Game, when, in examples (13) and (14), 'he', 'there' and 'it' substitute for whole phrases.

This kind of economy could lead to ambiguity: Who, precisely, is arguing and just who is sitting on what, eating what? Such non-specific language should not be risked in, say, instruction booklets: imagine trying to fathom the workings of a new word processor, or a washing machine, if the manual simply said 'Take that and turn it to there'.

Still, meaning will not be in doubt if the hearer is helped out by references made earlier in the written or spoken text. If the sentence, 'The hippo was sitting on the television', is followed by, 'He was eating a cheeseburger there', we know that 'there' refers to – substitutes for – 'on the television'. This is an example of *cohesion*, when one element of a set of utterances can only be understood by reference to another. Such links bind the text together as a single entity, a single structure that can be bigger than an individual sentence. Blake (1990: 104–21) includes a very helpful chapter on cohesion.

The word 'there' is, of course, a *preposition*. It is substituting for a *locative* phrase. But it is not essential, in order to make the Game's main Point that structure matters, for students to be able to recognize and name individual elements of syntax. Still, the Game might encourage students to do so (and they will certainly need explicit knowledge and metalanguage if they are to read about the Chomsky debate). If so, *Rediscover Grammar with David Crystal* (Crystal 1988) would be a helpful text for older students.

However, structuring is not the only significant feature of human communication. Some of these 'design features' are referred to in **Signing** (1.1) (drawing on Hockett and Altmann 1968), but they are collected together here for convenience and because they relate to the theme of 'humanness'. Whilst other creatures may possess some but not all of these features, no human language, by definition, is without any of them. In this sense, no language can be described as primitive or inferior to another [an argument to be borne in mind when playing **Sounds Familiar** (2.2), **Cross Talk** (2.4), **Talking 'Proper'?** (2.6) and **Laying Down the Language Law** (2.9), or discussing pidgins and creoles].

A point to make first, however, is that – as we can see in **Signing** (1.1) when discussing the language system used by people with impaired hearing – the use of sound, though usual in human language, is *not* its essential, defining feature.

Something that is a significant, defining feature, though, [as we can also see when playing **Signing** (1.1)] is that human language symbols are generally *arbitrary*: they do not, apart from onomatopoeic words, match that to which they refer. Animals, on the other hand, tend to make signals which are more directly linked to their message: a crab conveys anger by extending a large claw, and if it is not quite so annoyed it merely raises a leg. But there are exceptions. Gulls, for example, convey aggression in a less obvious way, by pulling up grass in their beaks. So arbitrariness is not *the* defining feature of human language.

Signing (1.1) also demonstrates that human language symbols have fairly precise *semanticity*. That is, they are imbued with meaning. So we can talk about a headache, a migraine, a hangover – but animals can, on the whole, only miaow, growl or signify distress in some other very general way without precisely labelling it. Still, a threatened vervet monkey makes different sounds depending on the kind of animal that is disturbing it: a chutter for a snake, a rraup for an eagle, a chirp for lions or leopards. So, though semanticity may be especially subtle and highly developed in human beings, we do not have exclusive ownership of this feature.

Then there is *displacement*. We can talk about things, events, ideas, in the past, present, future, or the abstract. Displacement is a potent capacity, for it helps us to imagine, theorize – and tell lies. But, as we can see in **Signing** (1.1), we are not entirely alone in this respect. Bees can 'talk' about the source of nectar even when they are a long way from it. But they have displacement in only a limited degree: they can refer only to nectar, and they do not appear to lie about its location!

Cultural transmission, passing language on from one generation to the next, is another feature of human communication. For although, as **Knowing the Rules** (1.3) explains, we seem to have an innate predisposition to acquire language, human beings have to be in what Chomsky has called a language-rich environment in order for this capacity to be triggered and developed. Other creatures may be able to acquire much of their system in isolation (isolated birds, for example, will generally sing recognizable songs, though these are almost always abnormal). Humans cannot.

However, once we have acquired the system, apparently from a combination of our innate predisposition with the stimulus of a language environment, we need never, ever, repeat the same sentence. We can say anything we wish: we do not merely (like parrots) copy utterances we have heard before. Because of language's design features – in particular, as we have seen, its complex structure dependence – we can, in theory, be infinitely creative, infinitely original, combining words and syntax in fresh ways and, even, inventing new vocabulary. Some animals can be taught to fill 'slots', but probably do not understand that one word can substitute for several. Washoe, the chimpanzee, did demonstrate some creativity. She could combine words into short sequences of her own invention (though, as we have seen, without necessarily ordering them significantly) and when she saw a swan she may have invented the sign 'waterbird'. On the other hand, she could have been making two separate signs to indicate two separate ideas: one for the water, the other for the swan itself. In human beings, however, there is no doubt that the design features of our language, especially our 'dependence' upon intricate structuring, gives each of us the potential to be *in*dependent, creative in a unique and powerful way.

Sequel

Poetry and patterning
Students might look more closely [here and in **Identikits** (1.4) and its Sequel] at an aspect of this creativity – this seeming paradox, that dependence can be a means of independence – in practice.

Poetry draws on precisely the same language systems, the same design features, as any other language behaviour. But it may use these resources particularly richly and, when it does, is a good example of the communicative potential we all possess, whether or not we are labelled 'poets' or 'artists'.

Given its own special scope for patterned form, for example, poetry may emphasize and use to the full [as in examples (a) and (b) below] the structural potential that is part and parcel of everyday language use.

(a) For instance, Emmett Williams's poem, 'do you remember' (1967: 322, and also with other exercises: Williams 1992), highlights the 'slots' of structure we mentioned above:

do you remember

do you remember

when i loved soft pink nights
and you hated hard blue valleys
and i kissed mellow red potatoes
and you loved livid green seagulls
and i hated soft yellow dewdrops
and you kissed hard pink oysters
and i loved mellow blue nights
and you hated livid red valleys
and i kissed soft green potatoes
and you loved hard yellow seagulls
and i hated mellow pink dewdrops
and you kissed livid blue oysters
and i loved soft red nights
and you hated hard green valleys
and i kissed mellow yellow potatoes
and you loved livid pink seagulls
and i hated soft blue dewdrops
and you kissed hard red oysters
and i loved mellow green nights
and you hated livid yellow valleys
and i kissed soft pink potatoes
and you loved hard blue seagulls
and i hated mellow red dewdrops
and you kissed livid green oysters
and i loved soft yellow nights
and you hated hard pink valleys
and i kissed mellow blue potatoes
and you loved livid red seagulls
and i hated soft green dewdrops
and you kissed hard yellow oysters
and i loved mellow pink nights
and you hated livid blue valleys
and i kissed soft red potatoes
and you loved hard green seagulls
and i hated mellow yellow dewdrops
and you kissed livid pink oysters
and i loved soft blue nights
and you hated hard red valleys
and i kissed mellow green potatoes
and you loved livid yellow seagulls
and i hated soft pink dewdrops

and you kissed hard blue oysters
and i loved mellow red nights
and you hated livid green valleys
and i kissed soft yellow potatoes
and you loved hard pink seagulls
and i hated mellow blue dewdrops
and you kissed livid red oysters
and i loved soft green nights
and you hated hard yellow valleys
and i kissed mellow pink potatoes
and you loved livid blue seagulls
and i hated soft red dewdrops
and you kissed hard green oysters
and i loved mellow yellow nights
and you hated livid pink valleys
and i kissed soft blue potatoes
and you loved hard red seagulls
and i hated mellow green dewdrops
and you kissed livid yellow oysters
and i loved soft pink nights?

This poem is actually one long sentence and its regular patterning throws into relief rules of English sentence structure: particular syntactic slots belong to certain places in a sentence, but any word can occupy these places if it is the appropriate part of speech and so 'fits' the slot. It is a bit like those railway station chocolate machines. You pull out a bar and another one, suitably shaped, falls down to take its place. This particular sentence consists of a main clause ('do you remember') followed by several subordinate clauses (introduced by the conjunction 'when', each of them linked by the conjunction 'and'), all of which include the following:

subject pronoun (e.g. *I*), verb (*loved*), object noun phrase consisting of two pre-modifying adjectives (*soft pink*) before a head word (*nights*).

Students know, more or less unconsciously, that these syntactic elements, in this order, follow rules of English grammar. But they may not be familiar with the related metalanguage used above and in the following paragraphs. However, the regular repetition of the poem's basic clause structure could help them to understand and learn the relevant labels. If this is a prime reason for playing **We're Only Human** (1.2), over and above acquainting students with the concept of structure in a general way, it might be useful to try **Knowing the Rules** (1.3) first. Then, Crystal (1988) is, particularly for older students, a very helpful text to develop metalanguage. Advanced students might consider the *transitivity* structure of the clauses, and the difference between the physical action of kissing and the mental processes of loving and hating. If so, they might be interested in Halliday (1973, esp. ch. 5), Halliday (1985, ch. 5) or Morley (1985).

As it happens, Williams chooses to rotate the words that fill his syntactic slots in unwavering sequences. The past-tense verbs 'loved', 'hated' and 'kissed' are the only ones used and they always appear in this order. The subject position 'slot' in the subordinate clauses alternates between the pronouns 'i' and 'you'. The object slot is occupied by one of the nouns, 'nights', 'valleys', 'potatoes', 'seagulls', 'dewdrops' or 'oysters', in this order. The first pre-modifying adjective in each noun phrase is selected from 'soft', 'hard', 'mellow' and 'livid', and they appear in this sequence, describing the second adjectives, which are all colours, taken in order from the list 'pink', 'blue', 'red', 'green' and 'yellow'. The first and the last selections from these options (on the second and the last line of the poem) match.

Students could try observing their own 'slot filling' creativity. And, naturally, they need not confine themselves to their creativity in writing poetry. Describing prose in terms of its 'slots', particularly everyday prose, would emphasize this aspect of our constant creative structure dependence.

Of course, the students are not likely to find themselves having filled slots in a routine vocabulary sequence, like Williams. His deliberate lexical regularity, choosing in a 'rule-governed' sequence from finite lists, is a patterning peculiar to this particular poem. It is not related to any of the regular rules of English we share and use habitually. But we could still say the sequencing is part of the poem's grammar – its own individual 'grammar'. For *grammars* are merely descriptions, or 'models', of the rules that are followed by a particular language or text. In this sense, there are as many English grammars as there are consistent varieties [and so regular Non-standard versions of English are as grammatical in their own right as the Standard variety, a point made in, for instance, **Talking 'Proper'?** (2.6), and a reason for the Kingman Report's insistence that the Standard should not replace other varieties but should be added to repertoires]. Students might like to explore the concept of a grammar of a text further. If so, they would find Traugott and Pratt (1980: 24–9) helpful.

(b) As for the way in which 'chunks' of structure belong in relationship to each other, and seem to have an invisible, underlying organization, students could look at e.e. cummings's poem 'Buffalo Bill'. (I am grateful to Ronald Chan, Loughborough University of Technology, for drawing my attention to the syntax and semantics of e.e. cummings's poetry.)

Buffalo Bill's
defunct
            who used to
            ride a watersmooth-silver
                                    stallion
and break onetwothreefourfive pigeonsjustlikethat
                                    Jesus

he was a handsome man
                        and what i want to know is
how do you like your blueeyed boy
            Mister Death   (Firmage 1981: 90)

It is conceivable, largely because there is no guiding punctuation to fix its structural organization, that this poem could be read aloud in at least two ways, suggesting different meanings. Rhythm and intonation can link together one, or another, set of possible syntactic groups, changing the poem's meaning in the process. For example, is the 'blueeyed boy' actually called 'Mister Death'? Who, then, is 'you'? Or – given that we can say/write phrases in a particular order, yet know in our mind that they have that invisible structure mentioned above, holding allegiance to phrases elsewhere in the structure – could 'Mister Death' be a phrase which belongs with (is in *apposition* to) 'you': 'how do you, Mister Death, like your blueeyed boy'? In the same sort of way, is 'who used to ride a watersmooth-silver stallion' a post-modifying relative clause that really belongs to the noun phrase of which 'Buffalo Bill' is head? It very likely is – but, as there is no punctuation to fix the matter, 'who' could, alternatively, herald the start of a new sentence structured in question form.

Common sense is likely to prefer one particular reading of this poem, and so it is not profitable, in terms of literary criticism, to spend a great deal of time discussing unlikely alternatives. However, students might use the exercise as a relatively straightforward forerunner to reading Gerard Manley Hopkins's poetry, helping them to appreciate Hopkins's work by describing its syntactic structures, and their complex relationships within sentences.

Those students who are secure in their understanding of syntax might then look, as in the Sequel to **Identikits** (1.4), at the meaningful subtleties of Cummings's lexical and syntactic choices in his poem 'anyone lived in a pretty how town' (Firmage 1981: 515).

Afterword

Game plan

Tupton Hall School found **We're Only Human** (1.2) worked well, especially when players were asked to form a specific number of changed structures, or when they were given the first word or phrase of possible alternatives. This helped to focus discussion and, presumably, helped students to get started.

Tutor and student comment

Tupton Hall School recommended, as a related exercise, the computer game *Wordplay*. The computer is given a variety of syntactic structures. Students type in lists of nouns, verbs, adjectives, and so on, or phrases instead of single words. The computer then creates poems, combining the words with the structures.

1.3 KNOWING THE RULES

Focus: Game 1.3 plays with lines from Lewis Carroll's 'Jabberwocky' with two Points in mind: (a) to dispel anxieties about the rules of syntax and morphol-

ogy by demonstrating to students that, without necessarily realizing it, they
have known these rules since they were very young, and (b) to explain, particularly with regard to language acquisition, what Chomsky has called rule-based
'competence' and to compare this with what Hymes (1971) has termed 'communicative competence'. The alternative to this Game plays with some of
these ideas through French and German translations of 'Jabberwocky'.

Age range: This game could be played at virtually any age to demystify syntax
[Point (a)]. Tupton Hall School found it suitable for 11–18 year olds. But it is
particularly intended to reassure older students, in Further and Higher Education, who at the present time might not have had much grounding in grammar and who are therefore particularly anxious about learning and remembering
its rules. Once confidence is gained, these older students will find a text like
Rediscover Grammar with David Crystal (Crystal 1988) helpful. The Game's
secondary aim, (b), is probably most appropriate for students aged 16 and over.

Preparation time: Nil.

Related Games: **Jigsaw Puzzles** (1.5), **Shaping Thought** (2.7)

The Game

The students, having first been reassured that this is not a test of their drawing
ability, are invited to sketch (individually or as a small group effort) whatever they imagine when they hear the following lines from Lewis Carroll's
'Jabberwocky' (*Through the Looking Glass* 1958: 154–6, first published in 1872):

'Twas brillig, and the slithy toves
  Did gyre and gimble in the wabe.

Alternative Game

Teachers of foreign languages might play a version of this game with advanced
students using translations of 'Jabberwocky's' first two lines. The French
extract given below is by Frank L. Warrin Jr, published in the *New Yorker* (10
January 1931). The German is by Dr Robert Scott, and appeared in *Macmillan's
Magazine* in February 1872. The complete translations of both (together with
a further, Russian, version) may be found in Norwich (1982: 213–15):

Il brilgue: les tôves lubricilleux
Se gyrent en vrillant dans le guave,

Es brillig war. Die schlichten Toven
  Wirrten und wimmelten im Waben;

Using these lines would not, of course, help English-speaking students to
recognize English syntactic knowledge they had always possessed – which is
the essential Point of the Game – but the exercise would still emphasize the

importance, to meaningful creativity, of word order and of morphological structure.

The Point of the Game

(a) If students have had little grounding in syntax – as could be the case if they were at Junior school before the Kingman initiatives – they may be confused by the terminology of grammar and afraid that it will always remain a mystery. This anxiety stands in the way of remedial work. But **Knowing the Rules** (1.3) is designed to dispel fear and, building confidence, to pave the way for the acquisition of a more explicit understanding of syntax, which will be useful to students in their analysis and evaluation of language (as discussed in Chapter 1). For playing the Game should prove to participants that they already – without necessarily being aware of it, without having the metalanguage to label it – possess a considerable amount of syntactic knowledge, including the rules of English word order and [a Point developed in **Jigsaw Puzzles** (1.5)] the internal, morphological structure of words. In other words, we are all grammatical experts! Indeed, all human beings are experts in their own particular language, each of which shares the kind of defining features discussed in **We're Only Human** (1.2) including, most importantly, a 'structure dependence' which is based upon *rules*. These are not rules of taste, decided upon by a language's most authoritative users in order to ensure their idea of consistent elegance: all varieties of a language, whether or not they conform to the version used by its most powerful and prestigious speakers, work by rule.

For example, it is likely that all the sketches produced in **Knowing the Rules** (1.3) will have similar ingredients; a number of creatures – very probably slimy and/or slithery – doing something, in something. But, since the poem's words are mostly nonsense, not part of the English lexicon, the question arises: How did the students arrive at similar pictures? Part of the answer has to be the very reassuring fact that they 'know' the rules of English syntax.

To begin with, the students evidently know they should draw some sort of 'thing' – in fact, more than one thing: 'toves'. This is presumably because 'toves' occurs soon after 'the' and partly because it ends in 's'. That is, because of the word's position in the utterance, and because of its internal form – its morphemic structure [see also **Jigsaw Puzzles** (1.5)] – players are at some level aware, without necessarily having learned the name of the word class, that 'toves' is acting as a noun and a plural noun at that. English-speaking students 'know' the rules that 'toves' is following. They can decode its structural signals.

Moreover, players are likely to have some idea of how the toves look. They must then have recognized 'slithy' as a modifier, or adjective, describing the toves. They will very likely agree they did so partly because 'slithy' is following rules of English word order, positioned as it is before the noun and after 'the', and also because of its 'y' ending, typical of a large number of English adjectives.

[The precise meaning of 'slithy' is another matter. No doubt the semantics of similar sounding English words, and probably onomatopoeia, play a part here. Actually, Humpty Dumpty told Alice (Carroll 1958: 222) it is a 'portmanteau' word, with two meanings 'packed' into it – lithe and slimy.]

So just these two brief examples suggest that – as a 'rule', and largely unconsciously, without necessarily having a descriptive metalanguage – we 'know' English word classes, and we 'know' what they are doing, either through their position in a sentence and/or via their own internal morphemic structures. This idea can be developed around more questions about the 'Jabberwocky' drawings. For instance, how did the sentence position of 'wabe' affect its representation in the drawings? Presumably, students know it is a noun word partly because it follows a determiner, in this case a definite article, 'the'.

Then, what response was there, in the drawings, to 'brillig'? Nine times out of ten the word guides students to draw a sunny day. Why? Probably they do so in part because the sound of 'brillig' resembles 'brilliant'. And they generally take it as an adjective – a descriptive word, a modifier of some kind – because, linking with the verb 'to be', it follows the pattern of familiar structures like 'It was cloudy' or 'It was sunny'. They could, however, like Humpty Dumpty, take 'brillig' to be a noun. For they might have in their minds English structures like 'it was + noun', e.g. 'it was lunchtime'. Humpty certainly did, for he thought 'brillig' referred to 'four o'clock in the afternoon – the time when you begin *broiling* things for dinner' (Carroll 1958: 222).

Next, how did the students know they should draw their toves doing something? In other words, why, even if they were not familiar with the grammatical terminology, did they take 'gyre' and 'gimble' to be verbs? Probably they made this decision because 'gyre' and 'gimble' are associated with 'did' ('did gyre, did gimble') and English users know that 'did' is, as a rule, involved with words which are verbs, or 'doing' words. True, most dialects of English would nowadays only hear 'did' in a question form ('Did you dance? Did you skip? Did you gyre? Did you gimble?') or else in answer to this form of question ('I did'). But 'they did dance, skip, gyre or gimble', on the other hand, is a more archaic form (or else a rather unusual, present-day, Non-standard dialect variation). Even so, students are recognizing 'did' as an 'auxiliary' to the main verb. They must certainly 'know' a great deal of grammar if they can deal not only with current usage but also with unusual, dated forms!

Yet I mentioned in the introduction some people's concern that certain users of English do *not* know any grammar. The Game demonstrates that this is an impossibility. A 'grammar' [as **We're Only Human** (1.2) also explains] is really only a 'model', a description of the rules of a language. To speak any language we must have internalized the grammar of our particular language. True, that grammar may represent the Standard or a Non-standard variety of a language – but, either way, it consists, by definition, of a set of rules to which its speaker regularly adheres. Those who know the rules of the Standard grammar may well not know the rules of Non-standard varieties (which accounts for some of their mistaken arguments against the Non-standard).

Part (a) of this Game stands alone as a demonstration that we do all possess language knowledge, whether or not we have been taught a metalanguage to articulate it explicitly. But where has our knowledge of a grammar come from? Why do we all know one? Students wishing to address these particular questions should consider Part (b) of the Game's Point.

(b) People's knowledge of their first language is not like their knowledge of a foreign language. If we learn the latter in school, we do so consciously (often painfully consciously!) and we could talk about what we have learned through the metalanguage that was used to teach us. For instance, if we take French as a second language, we are taught that generally we have to alter the ends of nouns, often by adding 's', if we want to convert them from singular to plural. We follow this rule knowingly: we ask ourselves, 'Should we add an 's' to this particular word or not?'

English, as our first language, is a different matter. We need, like the French, to be able to mark nouns as plural in some way. Like the French we do so, frequently though not always, by adding an 's'. But, unlike our acquisition of French, we come to know the rules of English while we are very young and we do so without formal training. Moreover, we carry on marking plural nouns all our adult lives – but without necessarily being able to talk about what we do (unless, as with French, we have had school grammar lessons somewhere along the way).

So, how *did* each of us 'learn' our first language, be it English, French, Swahili, Japanese or whatever, without formal tuition? How did we English speakers discover, without someone telling us, that we often make plurals by changing word endings? And how did speakers of Swahili learn to do something different, adding special prefixes to nouns, depending upon whether they are singular or plural and, also, upon whether they are animate or inanimate, e.g. basket/baskets = *ki*kapu/*vi*kapu, child/children = *m*toto/*wa*toto? (Students might like to follow this up through an exercise in Fromkin and Rodman 1988: 158–89.)

Possible answers to these questions come from the American linguist, Noam Chomsky. He is often said to have revolutionized thinking about language, particularly about language acquisition. Chomsky (1959) disagreed with B.F. Skinner (1957) who argued that we acquire our first language rather like caged laboratory rats. These animals, stimulated by hunger, learn by experience to press bars for food. Press the wrong bar and they are disappointed. Press the right one and food appears in their cage. Skinner thought we gained language knowledge in much the same way, by trial and error, punishment and reward. That is, if children find that using a particular bit of language works for them, gets them what they want, then they are rewarded and will try the same strategy again.

Chomsky insisted this argument was too simplistic. In the first place, language is far more complex than a few easily predictable 'operations', stimulated by specific circumstances. For instance, unlike the rat who is limited to one particular bit of behaviour, a child who is stimulated by hunger may say any number of things: 'I want a biscuit' or 'Have we any crisps?' or 'My tummy hurts', etc. Besides, a child who is *not* hungry, but merely wants to delay bedtime, may also say any or all of these things! For human beings are, linguistically, infinitely creative. In theory we need never repeat the same sentence from now until the end of our lives. And we are not parrots, merely storing up a bank of suitable sentences to be repeated according to circumstance. On the contrary, our knowledge includes rules from which we can make up utterances we have never heard before. So the hungry child might insist, 'Our head teacher said, "Tell your mother you are always to eat Chinese take-away with your homework".' I doubt if this sentence had been heard before and memorized!

Furthermore, unlike the rat/bar experiment, there is no single, predictable response to the hungry child's utterance, whatever form it takes. Food may be forthcoming, or it may not. Yet the 'punishment' of denial will not necessarily deter the child from trying the same linguistic strategies on another occasion.

Chomsky also thinks it significant, in arriving at a theory of language acquisition, that children seem to gain the infinite creativity of their first language in apparently unfavourable circumstances. Imagine a toddler in a high chair, surrounded by siblings shouting, parent answering the telephone, the television on in the background. How is it that – from this jumbled model (so much more complex than the rat/cage/bar situation) and at this age before intelligence is fully developed – we can acquire the intricacies of our particular language (English if we are surrounded by English, Swahili if that is spoken around us, and so on)? How do we do so with such ease, so much more comfortably than most of us acquire our second language at school? Nobody sits down with us when we are toddlers and tests us on vocabulary. Nobody tells us how to turn present-tense verbs into past, actives into passives, and so on. In fact, when teachers take the time and trouble to point these things out at school, we often find them far more difficult to grasp consciously than we did, unconsciously, as young children. Why?

Chomsky believes that the answers to such questions depend upon the human possession of a special knowledge, i.e. *competence*. He argues that we are born ready to develop this 'competence' so long as we grow up surrounded by language. He has suggested, for instance, that we are born knowing how to distinguish the sounds of language from other non-linguistic sounds (like sneezes). And he has argued that we have an in-built 'hypothesis-making' device, an innate facility which helps us to test out the 'rules' we suspect we have discovered in our language, rules of syntax which, once learned, allow us the infinite creativity mentioned above. It is rather like learning to work with Lego bricks. We recognize them as bricks and we know there must be some significant way of putting them together. Once we have worked out, from observing others playing with them, that the bricks can be stuck together, top to bottom – once we have learned this simple structural rule – we can create from them anything we choose: a house, a farm, soldiers, robots, dogs, cats.

For instance, imagine the small girl who, for weeks, has been saying 'Mummy went work', and then think of her parents' consternation when she suddenly switches to 'Mummy goed work'. Chomskyans would reassure her parents that she has not regressed. On the contrary, she is demonstrating that she is developing her linguistic 'competence': she has internalized a rule of her speech community's language. For it would appear that when this little girl was saying 'went' she was merely parroting what she had heard others say. But when she changed to 'goed' she had used her hypothesis-making device. She had hypothesized that, *as a rule*, her speech community makes past tenses by adding 'ed' and, for the time being, until she learns the exceptions to this structural rule (like 'went'), she is simply over-extending a practice that in general she has found to work. From now on, this child will be able to make any past-tense verb that follows the '+ ed' shape, whether or not she has actually heard someone else use it. She is no longer parroting. She is acquiring the structural rules of language, developing her innate facility for language and doing so on a schedule that roughly matches other children of English-speaking families. Indeed, it would appear that children the world over acquire the rules of their particular language in a similar sequence (and there may be a crucial period beyond which it is much more difficult to begin acquisition – a partial explanation, perhaps, of problems in learning second languages, later on, at school).

Not every linguist agrees with the details of Chomsky's argument (and, of course, his own thinking continues to develop). Some have a different view of the precise kind of linguistic knowledge we may be born with. But probably most would accept that we do have an innate predisposition of some sort, something quite apart from intelligence. For even highly intelligent animals, like chimpanzees, though they may be helped to acquire certain aspects of language, do not seem capable of the immense human creativity which depends upon manipulating the structures of language according to a set of internalized rules.

Our knowledge of syntax, giving us this infinite creativity, helps us to 'mean' – and to mean in subtle ways. Stylistic analysis demonstrates this and is the Point of the Game, **Shaping Thought** (2.7). This Game begins by looking at the meaningful choices of language in newspapers. However, it is not only journalists, but all of us, who can manipulate syntax and other aspects of language, in order to encourage the way others see things. To take a relatively trivial example, how often have we heard children (and ourselves!) avoiding responsibility by saying, as they hold a smashed plate, 'It slipped' – not 'I dropped it' or even 'It was dropped'. The plate has, through these choices of syntax, become the agent of its own destruction. How fortunate it is that we know so much about language – and learn how to put it into practice!

For when we have developed competence, internalizing the rules of our particular speech community's language and building up what, roughly, the Swiss linguist, Saussure, termed *langue*, we need still more knowledge in order to use our language effectively, in society. We need 'rules' of a different kind in order to achieve what Chomsky has called *performance* and Saussure termed *parole*. We shall need to know, for instance, how to make conversation according to our culture's conventions, how to talk to our friends, to colleagues, to employers, how to write essays, how to write letters, and so on. Actually, 'conventions' might be a better word than rules here, for these can, more readily than the rules of competence, be broken without total loss of comprehension.

Dell Hymes (1971) has called this the acquisition of *communicative competence*. So, does it follow that we are *in*competent if we flout these conventions? Who establishes them? How often, in practice, are they disregarded, and to what effect? Putting language into performance, through our communicative competence – and wondering precisely what constitutes 'effective', 'appropriate' performance, and how much individual choice we have in the matter – is a central theme of games like **Variety Performance** (2.1), **Talking Power** (2.3) and **Cross Talk** (2.4).

Afterword

Tutor and student comment
Tupton Hall School staff developed this Game by constructing other 'nonsense' sentences, for analysis, and getting the students to do likewise. Some of their sentences – like 'The goldiblee uffleflugged the bolliplobs' – threaten to beat Lewis Carroll and Humpty Dumpty at their own game!

1.4 IDENTIKITS

Sequel: **Breaking the rules**

(I am indebted to Lucy Shepherd for suggesting this Game and its applications.)

Focus: Practice in labelling word classes and syntactic structures, with some reference to semantics and, in the Sequel, to literary criticism.

Age range: Juniors upwards.

Preparation time: Suitable syntactic structures will need to be decided on prior to the Game. Examples of e.e. cummings's poetry would be needed for the Sequel.

Related Games: **Knowing the Rules** (1.3) (it might be helpful to play this first as it is designed mainly to dispel anxiety about grammar) and **Jigsaw Puzzles** (1.5) are relevant. **Identikit's** link with literature [Point (c)] anticipates the discussion of 'stylistics' in **Shaping Thought** (2.7) and in **Form and Focus** (2.8).

The Game

Staff should write the structure of a sentence on the board. For example:

Determiner, pre-modifier, noun, verb, determiner, pre-modifier, pre-modifier, noun.

The structure chosen will of course vary in type and complexity according to the aspect of grammar you wish to teach (see Point of the Game). Also, the metalanguage you use may vary. I am using *determiner* to refer to any word which can precede a noun and determine the number and definiteness of the noun. I am using pre-modifier to refer to any word which can go between the determiner and the noun. The noun may be called the *head word* of a *noun phrase*, which can include determiners and pre-modifiers preceding the head word and, following it, *post-modifiers*. This terminology is in line with that used in Crystal (1988).

Players should divide up into groups: the number in each group will be the same as the number of words that would fit into the sentence pattern on the board (eight in the case of the example given above). Each group needs a sheet of paper and a pencil.

The first person in the group should, privately, write down on the piece of paper a word that fits the first class of word given on the board – a determiner, in the case of the given example. This player should then fold the paper over so that the word cannot be seen and pass it on to the next person. The second player should now respond to the second class of word on the board. In the case of the given example, he or she should write down a pre-modifier (without reference to the previously chosen determiner) and then fold the paper over and pass it on. The procedure should be repeated – a bit like Chinese Whispers – until the whole structure on the board has been dealt with.

Finally, the piece of paper should be opened and the sentence written there should be read out. When we tried it, we discovered that one group of players had written:

The striped dustbin embraced a pink tasty giraffe.

The Point of the Game

A number of Points (relating to metalanguage, linguistic theory, semantics) may be made, depending partly on the age of the players. The Game's Sequel extends these to literary criticism.

(a) *Structures, classes and metalanguage.* The simplest Point of this Game is that words fit into 'family' groups (which we can label with a metalanguage) and we are accustomed to arranging words from these families in certain patterns. [The Sequel that follows **We're Only Human** (1.2) plays with the same Point with the help of a poem by Emmett Williams.] If a group has chosen the right kind of word – selected from the right family for the right place in the pattern – a point can be awarded (and so, if you wish, a competitive element can be built into the Game). If the sentence sounds odd, however, the wrong class of word may have been slotted into the structure. [Of course, the 'oddness' could be semantic, not syntactic. This is discussed in (b) immediately below, and also in the Game's Sequel.] In the following, a noun has been put where a verb was asked for, and it certainly sounds out of place:

The striped dustbin *deckchair* a pink tasty giraffe.

In the same way (hence the title of the Game), an Identikit picture would be useless if the person assembling it puts an ear in the place where a nose was asked for.

(b) *Syntagms and paradigms.* Students might like to think further about this structured patterning of syntax. They could be introduced to the notion of *syntagm* and *paradigm*.

Utterances come out of our mouths, or are written down, in strings. Imagine the string, the combination or 'syntagm', of words that comes out of the comic book character's mouth and into the bubble the cartoonist draws emerging from a figure's lips. If the words go in the wrong place on the syntagm, their meaning is blurred or destroyed [as we saw above and also in **We're Only Human** (1.2)]: 'The cat sat on the mat' is meaningful but 'Cat the on sat mat the' is not.

However, the meaningful combinations of syntagms do not leave their speakers/writers without choices. Each word 'slot' along the syntagm provides us with plenty of scope, for we can choose any word that 'fits' the slot [as **We're Only Human** (1.2b) demonstrates through a poem by Emmett Williams]. It will fit if it belongs to the right 'paradigm', or pile of words appropriate to that slot. Imagine one of those chocolate machines with a pile of chocolate bars – we might say a 'paradigm' of bars – stacked up inside it. We put the right money in, a bar falls down, we take it out of the machine and another of the same shape descends to take its place.

But the new bar must be the right shape or it will not fit the slot. And if words are not the right syntactic 'shape', they too will not fit. In the following example, *cat*, *mouse* and *judge* are all nouns, so can all fit in the same noun slot:

The *cat* sat.
The *mouse* sat.
The *judge* sat.

But the groups of words below will not do because the noun slot has been filled in each case by a word from the wrong family paradigm:

The *and* sat.
The *squelchy* sat.
The *could* sat.

However, words might fit syntactically but still seem peculiar, out of place. Take for example 'telephoned' in

The cat telephoned.

It does not seem quite right. At least, though a cat might well make telephone calls in a child's story book world, the idea of one placing a call in the real world is odd. Even odder would be:

The fireplace telephoned.

This is even more peculiar than the cat sentence because at least cats are animate – they do 'live' things, even though we do not expect them to do human things. But fireplaces, being inanimate, are not expected to be active in any way at all.

In both cases, then, as 'telephoned' is a verb, it fits perfectly into the syntagm *syntactically*, but it is *semantically* odd. We could say that there is a mismatch between the *semantic properties* that speakers of English would usually agree belong to 'cat' and 'fireplace' and those they would agree belong to 'telephoned'. Among its properties 'cat', as we have already established, has 'animate', 'fireplace' has 'inanimate' and 'telephoned' assumes a human user.

If students wish to read about semantics, there is a very helpful chapter in Fromkin and Rodman (1988: 205–250).

Sequel

Breaking the rules
Of course, semantic oddness does not always disqualify a word from filling a particular slot. We can sometimes accommodate oddness and frequently do so in specially creative writing like poetry. So students might like to use this Game as a forerunner to close reading and literary criticism, assessing how far the words they have accidentally chosen in **Identikits** (1.4) – odd or otherwise – are, in some sense, appropriate in their slots. For because these choices have been made in the dark, as far as associated meaning is concerned, the Game is likely to produce interesting, sometimes very strange, semantic packages. And players may feel more relaxed about debating the implications and effectiveness of words and phrases (what is a dustbin doing embracing a giraffe, and in any case can you have pink giraffes, let alone pink and tasty ones?) in these uncontrolled and often amusing mixes than they frequently do, at least to begin with, in the sacrosanct stanzas and paragraphs of the established canon.

However, this exercise is not intended to give the impression the 'oddness' is an essential prerequisite of literary choice: it is suggested merely as a way into talking about language choices, from the clearly unusual to the less obviously striking.

Having done so with regard to their **Identikit** sentences, more advanced students, secure in their basic understanding of syntax and semantics, might go on to think about the work of e.e. cummings, which so frequently challenges our conventional semantic and syntactic expectations. Take, for example, his poem, 'anyone lived in a pretty how town' (Firmage 1981: 515). It includes lines like

> he sang his didn't he danced his did

and

> busy folk buried them side by side
> little by little and was by was

and

> and more by more they dream their sleep
> noone and anyone earth by april
> wish by spirit and if by yes

Students might decide that these odd syntactic and semantic choices have no significance apart from curiosity value. But, in the context of the whole poem, they are more likely to make out a very different case, arguing that cummings's inventive structuring is profoundly meaningful. This kind of language analysis, 'stylistic' criticism, is picked up and developed in **Shaping Thought** (2.7) and in **Form and Focus** (2.8).

If students do find 'anyone lived in a pretty how town' subtly meaningful, how do they do so? Do they rapidly recall a word's conventional syntactic and semantic use, then add this 'meaning' to a significance that the place it now occupies usually implies? Does 'how', normally an interrogative adverb but appearing here in an adjective slot, somehow add a questioning gloss to 'pretty' and maybe to 'town'? Does the 'nouning' of 'didn't', normally part of a verb phrase, emphasize the active nature of that newly created 'noun'? Clearly something unusual is going on with regard to the comprehension of cummings's work, but for a discussion of the way in which we may comprehend more usual everyday structures, see Aitchison (1989: 241–61).

Afterword

Tutor and student comment
Although **Identikits** (1.4) begins with the trappings of children's party entertainment, mature students who have, to begin with, very little syntactic metalanguage, find it an enjoyable bridge to much more sophisticated language discussion and literary criticism.

1.5 JIGSAW PUZZLES

Sequel: **Politic words**

Focus: The word-building rules of derivational and inflectional morphology (1.5A,B) related to the poetry of G.M. Hopkins (1.5C) and, in the Sequel, to the words of feminism and of Rastafarian language.

Age range: Game 1.5A could be adapted to any age. Game 1.5B is designed for 14 plus. Game 1.5C, and also the Sequel, are most suitable for students aged 16 and over. However, Games 1.5B and C, and of course the Sequel, should not be tried until after the Point of the Game has been discussed [and, as usual, this will not happen until the basic Game (1.5A) has been played].

Preparation time: Relevant sentences and words might be photocopied in advance (for 1.5A and perhaps 1.5B), but these could be written on the board. Extracts from G.M. Hopkins will be needed for Game 1.5C.

Related Games: It would be helpful to play **Knowing the Rules** (1.3) in relation to its Point (a) before trying out **Jigsaw Puzzles**.

The Game (1.5A)

Students, playing in twos, should solve the following puzzle: What are the structural differences within and between the pairs of sentences given below, and what do these elements of structure 'mean'?

1(a) Snow White met the seven dwarfs who lived in a house with seven chairs and seven beds.

1(b) Snow White met the enseven endwarfo who lived in a house with seven little chairo and seven little bedo.

2(a) The glass slipper was tried by every young woman in the land.

2(b) The glass slipper was tried by every enyoung enwoman in the land.

The puzzle can be easily solved without much of the Point of the Game being explained. It would only be necessary, as they play, to remind students that, rather like doing jigsaw puzzles, we 'make' words by putting meaningful 'bits' of structure – or *morphemes* – together. For example, in English, we frequently construct plural words by adding the morpheme -*s* to the end of a singular word. It is a kind of *rule* that we follow, usually without conscious thought. So one 'chair' becomes two or more 'chairs', one 'bed' becomes a number of 'beds', and so on.

The first sentence of the first pair in the game is obviously in English: for one thing, its plurals follow this particular rule. The second sentence of this pair is, for the same reason, clearly not English. It is an invented language that we might call 'Morpho' for convenience and to draw attention to its morphological differences. This language would seem to make plurals by adding -*o* to the end of singular nouns: bedo, chairo.

By noting other differences within and between both pairs of sentences (sentence 2a is also clearly in English, sentence 2b is in Morpho), students can puzzle out two more of Morpho's morphological rules, reminding themselves, by contrast, of another aspect of English structure. That is, Morpho clearly displays two rules that English does not share. English does not, through structure, distinguish animate from inanimate nouns and related adjectives. Morpho does. It evidently begins nouns that are animate, and adjectives that describe animate nouns, with *en*-. Inanimate nouns, and related adjectives, have no such addition. Students could try translating other English sentences into Morpho, observing these simple rules.

Further explanations of morphology can be given, depending on the age of the pupils, after Game 1.5A has been played. Games 1.5B and 1.5C should not be played until the Point has been discussed.

The Point of the Game

(a) Words like 'structure' and 'rules' may sound unattractively restrictive [though Games like **Knowing the Rules** (1.3) demonstrate that this is not the case]. They do not obviously suggest links with imagination and flexibility, particularly to students bored with, or anxious about, grammar. Yet rule-governed morphology is no strait-jacket: it is a means to a creative end.

Morphemes are the smallest syntactic unit: a morphemic unit is always, in some sense, significant. Morphemes and syllables are not the same thing: syllables need not be significant, in that they need not have meaning in their own right. We sense that parts of words form 'chunks', each including a vowel sound, i.e. syllables. So we would say there are two syllables in 'kennel' (ken-nel), three syllables in 'furniture' (fur-ni-ture), and so on. But these particular syllables are not also morphemes because they are not syntactically significant, not intrinsically meaningful in some way. Sometimes, however, syllables also qualify as morphemes because they happen (as discussed below) to be meaningful in their own right.

Sometimes, a word consists of only one meaningful bit – one morpheme. These morphemes are called *free* morphemes, because they do not need to rely on any other morphemes in order to make sense. (They could be made up, like 'furniture', of more than one syllable.) For instance, the word 'dog' can exist quite independently. It does not need anything adding to it in order to be meaningful: it is a self-sufficient, free morpheme. Moreover, 'dog' cannnot be divided up into any more bits that have meaning relative to the animal: 'd' and 'og' mean nothing by themselves and, though 'do' (do-g) can have meaning, in this case it does not because it is not directly linked to the word's overall meaning of an animal with four legs, a tail and a bark. (This point may need emphasizing: students often find it difficult to grasp that morphemic meaning must relate to the particular word in question.)

However, if we add an -s to 'dog', we add *more* meaning: 'dogs'. If you are told to take the 'dog' for a walk, you know you are meant to set off with only one animal in tow. But if you are told to take the 'dogs', you know something else is meant: you are intended to go with at least two trotting along beside you. These additional morphemes are 'affixes' – bits fixed, or *bound*, on. If the affix comes at the end of a word, then it is a suffix. If it comes at the beginning, then it is a prefix.

The notion of 'meaning' is clearly rather odd in the case of bound morphemes like -s. We shall not find the meaning of -s defined in a dictionary. This is because -s is just like a bit of a jigsaw puzzle: unrecognizable on its own, but having significance when put in the right place in the completed jigsaw. For instance, if a teacher said

I want all those on the window side of the room using -s, those on the door side using -s.

the class would be mystified: -s is meaningless (unless the sentence implies 'I want all those on the window side of the room using the letter of the alphabet "s"'). However, add one -s to a morpheme/word like 'paint', the other to something like 'crayon', and everthing becomes clear.

I want all those on the window side of the room using paints, those near the door using crayons.

The point is that morphemes like -s are useless – meaningless – on their own. They must (in contrast to those 'free' morphemes, like 'dog', which can, in the right syntactic circumstances, act quite alone) be *bound* to another morpheme in order for their significance to be released.

(b) It can now be pointed out to older students (*before* playing Games 1.5B and 1.5C) that there are different ways of combining morphemes, different kinds of *morphology* that produce different kinds of syntactic significance and meaning. That is, there is *derivational* and there is *inflectional* morphology. These are *rule-based* systems of word creation. Their rules do not restrict language users but give us the potential to be infinitely inventive.

Morphemes like -s and -ed are said to *inflect* other morphemes. That is, they add some meaning to a word but they do not change the word syntactically or semantically in any fundamental way. A noun, or a verb, stays a noun or a verb despite being inflected. 'Dogs' remains a noun, fitting into the same place in the sentence, still referring to creatures with tails and barks, although 'dog' has been inflected and become plural. 'Walked' remains a verb, fitting into the same place in the sentence, even though 'walk' has been inflected to turn it from a present into a past tense.

I walk the dog before lunch.

I *walked* the *dogs* before lunch.

We know the rules behind these changes. We can represent them as follows:

singular noun + s = plural noun

basic form of the verb + ed = past-tense verb

We can operate these same rules and turn *label, suit, exam* and so on into plurals, *laugh, talk, gossip* into past tenses.

Derivational morphology, on the other hand, can, and often does, change a word syntactically. Take the word 'thin'. It is an adjective (the thin teacher), but add the morpheme -*ly* and we derive an adverb (smiled thinly). The rule is:

adjective + ly = adverb

The word class has changed, so the newly created adverb has to be slotted into a different part of the sentence from the original adjective. We could not refer to:

the thinly teacher.

We could only say something like

The thin teacher smiled thinly.

Derivational morphology does not always create different word classes in this sort of way. But it always makes a totally new word in some sense. 'Carthorse' is a word derived from 'cart' and 'horse'. Adding 'cart' to 'horse' makes something quite different in meaning from 'horse' – you would hardly race a carthorse in the Gold Cup – though the new word is still a noun, fitting into the same place in the sentence. The rule is:

noun + noun = (newly derived) noun

He rode the horse in the Gold Cup.

He rode the carthorse, harnessed to the dray.

Naturally, just to make life more interesting – or difficult – there are exceptions to morphological rules. Sometimes English pluralizes not at the end but in the middle of a word: 'goose' becomes 'geese'. Sometimes it does not make plurals that are distinctly different from singulars: 'sheep' can mean one or an infinite number of woolly animals. Plurals like these have to be learned individually.

Evidently, then, a morpheme can vary from its basic form. For instance, the plural morpheme -*s* can be pronounced in a number of ways. Try saying

dogs, giraffes, houses

All have the familiar plural morpheme added, but it sounds a bit different in each case. Each variation is called an *allomorph* of the plural morpheme.

Games 1.5B and 1.5C could now be played by older students.

The Game (1.5B) (particularly suitable with regard to inflectional morphology)

Students should divide into teams of about three or four. The teams should be given a very short poem, mini-story or brief description (a different piece of writing for each team) in English. Something like the nursery rhyme, Ba Ba Black Sheep, would do. An example of a mini-story could be:

> The Prince met the lovely Cinderella. She was wearing glass slippers and a satin gown. At midnight her fine clothes turned to rags but the Prince loved her forever.

(Teams could write their own sentences but staff will need to keep an eye on these to be sure they include material that is challenging but not too difficult.)

The teams should then translate their text into an *invented* language (something like Morpho, perhaps, but different again). That is, using English words as their starting point, students should adapt some of these to form a new language by inventing new, non-English, morphological (particularly inflectional) rules. They need not stick to adaptations of the sort of rules familiar to English speakers. They could do something like Swahili, for example, signalling the difference betweeen inanimate and animate nouns (the 'bags' and the 'sheep' of the nursery rhyme) with different prefix morphemes ('kibags', 'msheep'). Or, like the French, they could choose to signal gender, even when there is no biological distinction, by adding significant morphemes to some of the nouns in their piece and perhaps to related adjectives. They might even, in cases like Ba Ba Black Sheep, find a different way of structuring questions. They might, instead of inverting word order, add some sort of 'query' morpheme to the verb, e.g. 'You ka-have any wool?'

If the teams include speakers of other languages, apart from English, they could be asked to explain their own morphological rules and these might be adapted for the game.

Teams should then exchange their translated stories (without their English prototypes) and, having done so, they should translate the story they have just received back into English by working out and listing (following the form used in Game 1.5A, for example, noun + s = plural noun) the morphological rules of the invented language.

The Game (1.5C) (*re* derivational morphology)

Derivational morphology is a powerful source of creativity, and so it is not surprising to find it used in deeply meaningful ways in poetry. For instance,

Gerard Manley Hopkins's work is, in my view, enriched by a profound morphological inventiveness (Gardner 1953).

Students might like to:

1 Confirm, or challenge, this opinion by looking more closely at his poetry, and then
2 Try writing their own poetry in a way that depends for some of its significance on this kind of morphological creativity.

Frequently, Hopkins's inventiveness is particularly clear because he marks the join between yoked-together morphemes with a hyphen.

Sometimes he uses rules which, though they derive new words, do not change the classes of their original morphemes/words. For instance,

adjective + adjective = (newly derived) compound adjective

The rule produces compound words like

white-fiery . . . snow

('The Wreck of the Deutschland', Gardner 1953: 16)

Such combinations are often energized by a form of alliteration, matching the initial consonants of the original two words or morphemes:

blue-bleak embers

('The Windhover', ibid.: 30)

Similarly, Hopkins sometimes uses the rule

noun + noun = (newly derived) compound noun

as he does in

wind-walks

('Hurrahing in Harvest', ibid.: 31)

and in

neighbour-nature

('Duns Scotus's Oxford', ibid.: 40)

and, a particularly interesting one, in

'to his *selfbent* so bound . . .'

('Ribblesdale', ibid.: 51)

However, Hopkins also uses derivational morphology in a way that does affect word classes. He may implement the rule

adjective + noun = (newly derived) compound, working as an adjective

as he does in

wanwood leafmeal [itself a compound]

('Spring and Fall', ibid.: 50)

Or he may work with

verb + noun = adjective

as, I believe, he does in

dare-gale skylark

('The Caged Skylark', ibid.: 31)

('As a dare-gale skylark scanted in a dull cage
   Man's mounting spirit in his bone-house, mean house, dwells – ').

It is just possible that 'dare' could be defined as, in origin, a noun. Still, I suggest that, given the context of the poem, 'dare' feels more like a verb in origin and thus the newly derived adjective yokes together a sense of activity with a powerful force; in other words, the newly derived adjective-like compound suggests activity pitted against that force. That is, Hopkins encapsulates in one short compound a whole image: something like the skylark 'who normally dares the force of gales'.

In this sort of way, Hopkins's syntactic inventiveness adds to his poetry, time after time, layers of meaning that are, in their economy and originality of expression, particularly vital and rich.

Sequel

Politic words
Older students might consider the significant comparisons and contrasts that can be noted between English morphology and the feminist and Rastafarian approaches to word structure.

The word-building of both feminists and Rastafarians is, no doubt, inspired consciously or unconsciously by the model of language's morphological structuring. However, noting the differences between their word division and morphology, particularly derivational morphology, should be instructive – reinforcing, by contrast, the definition of the morpheme and also recalling some English morphemic rules and our knowledge of these rules.

So, working individually, or in small groups, students should decide first on the linguistic morphemic analysis of words like 'history', 'historian', 'historic' and 'therapy', 'therapist', 'therapeutic'. They will note that 'history' and 'therapy' are each one free morpheme (each of three syllables) and each of the derived words adds one more morpheme. Then they should think about a feminist division of 'history' into 'his-story' and 'therapist' into 'the-rapist' (Daly 1978) or the transformation, used by a number of feminists, of 'heroes' into 'sheroes'.

Students should next work out what is happening in the Rastafarian substitution of the word/morpheme 'I' in the following words:

creation becomes Iration

respect becomes Ispect

reconcile becomes Iconcile

control becomes Icontrol

recreate becomes Icreate

mediate becomes Idiate

These unusual feminist amd Rastafarian language manipulations are ideo-logically interesting. For instance, the feminist word play, quoted here, is intended to draw attention to women's marginalization and oppression. It is an effective tactic. But the manipulation does not isolate morphemes and then work on rules which could easily be extended to derive other, related words. 'His' and 'story', 'the' and 'rapist' were never, in 'history' and 'therapy', separable morphemes. In the contexts of these words, they are merely one or two syllables, without independent meaning. Of course, playing with syllables instead of morphemes does not in the least diminish the feminist challenge, a challenge which draws attention to the existence of female as well as male heroes, female as well as male history. But it is worth looking closely at this kind of creativity because the energy sometimes spent in denouncing 'his-(s)tory', on the ground that it was a word created by men to exclude women, is wasted on a linguistic red herring.

The Rastafarian approach is another deliberate, meaningful manipulation. It may work on morphemes or on syllables. Rastafarians (see Sutcliffe and Wong 1986) believe that language could be a powerful means of stressing the specialness of their particular form of Black culture. For reasoning and discussion are made possible through language. Moreover, its rhythms and sounds can draw attention to its message and also to its users. But Rastafarians feel – and they are surely right – that people usually take language for granted, not hearing all its signals, not consciously noticing its power. Therefore, they deliberately spotlight their own words, making them strange in significant ways.

For instance, Rastafarians argue that English is used in a classist and racist way because they believe that white people think of themselves as 'I', individuals of supreme importance, and regard black people as unimportant others: 'you', 'they'. The more Rastafarians can use 'I', therefore, the more symbolic power they draw to themselves. So, whenever possible, they substitute this morpheme for a word's first syllable. It goes in this first place consistently, because to be first is of premier importance (and 'I' itself is labelled 'first person' pronoun). But the consistency is not syntactic. For sometimes the replaced syllable is a morpheme, sometimes it is meaningless.

Another example of Rastafarian language manipulation is the elimination of 'hostile' sounds. Rastafarians believe that the syllable 'ate' in 'appreciate' is ugly – if for no other reason than that it sounds like 'hate' – and the word is thus self-contradicting, expressing something good in a hostile way. They would therefore prefer to say 'apprecilove', and 'congregation' could become 'congrelove'. However, Rastafarians prize quick-witted, original improvisation, so other substitutions are possible. For example, they might say 'congreman'. They would not choose 'congremen', though, because Rastafarians are unhappy with the word 'men'. For although 'man' is good (given 'The Son of man'), 'men' (given 'All sins shall be forgiven unto the sons of men': Mark 3.28) are not. Rastafarians will therefore eliminate the morpheme 'ment' from words like 'settlement', because it contains the syllable (not, of course, a morpheme in this case) 'men'. Instead they substitute 'man', i.e. 'settleman'. Similarly, they might choose to replace the first syllable of 'mental' and turn it into 'mantal'.

In summary, then, both feminist and Rastafarian word-building would seem to be inspired by the sort of structural creativity that is a defining feature of human language, but their inventiveness frequently achieves its provocative, thought-provoking signals by following rather different principles.

Afterword

Tutor and student comment
Older students usually appreciate the interdisciplinary relevance of parts of this Game. They find its application to literature (1.5C) interesting and they see links with the Sequel in a variety of subjects including sociology and psychology.

1.6 SOUNDS SUSPICIOUS

Focus: Transcribing consonant and vowel-type sounds using a phonetic alphabet.

Age range: From 14 years to Higher Education.

Preparation time: This is a difficult Game to set up and to carry out, at least for younger students. Time will be needed to arrange and make a brief tape-recording of one of the players – without the rest of the class knowing what is happening. The phonetic alphabet, given at the end in the Game Plan, will need photcopying. The fine details of the procedure in particular classrooms will also need working out beforehand (some general suggestions are made in the Game Plan following the Point of the Game). However, despite its difficulties, the Game can – with goodwill all round – be beneficial, so long as it is appreciated that its objectives are very basic and general. That is, it can demonstrate that phonetic transcription has its uses and can start students listening carefully with minimal anxiety.

Related Games: **Sound Sense** (1.7), **Sounds Familiar** (2.2), **Talking 'Proper'?** (2.6).

The Game

Before the class, unknown to the other students in the group, one of its members tapes something like the following:

> There's a woman 'urt. She's at 'arrison Road, number 5. I didn't mean to 'urt 'er. I only wanted 'er silver. She neeeds a hambulance. Har you listening? She needs a hambulance right away!

At the start of the class, the group (still not knowing that one of their number has made the recording) are told to imagine that someone has just broken into 5 Harrison Road. But as the burglar made an escape, the owner appeared on the scene. The burglar pushed past her, knocking her down in the process. The owner hit her head on the edge of a table and, fearing she may be seriously hurt, the intruder has phoned the police station to report the injury – though, naturally enough, not giving his or her name. The call – which the students should now hear – has been taped at the station.

The class should next divide into groups of about four and imagine themselves as detectives. If they could match the anonymous tape-recording with a sample of a suspect's voice, then these detectives would have some evidence on which to make an arrest and to offer in court. (It would not, in reality, be sufficient to obtain a conviction but could be offered as part of the case for the prosecution.) They should be told that, when they hear it, the voice on the tape will probably sound familiar: the speaker is quite famous. This is perfectly true! The student actor is well known to the class and in this sense famous. But since 'fame' is not usually associated with people close at hand, the remark should help to put everyone off the scent long enough for the game to be played.

The teams of detectives (one team unwittingly including in its midst the student who has made the recording) now listen to the tape and, using a copy of the alphabet given in the Game Plan below, help each other to transcribe the sounds of the call. The alphabet symbols are matched with words in ordinary script which give an indication of the sounds they represent. Players should be encouraged to take note of any consonant or vowel sounds which might be significant for the purposes of identification. The suggested script, with its 'dropped' and added /h/, is designed to make this relatively easy [but see Game Plan (b), below].

Having done their transcripts, students can now be told that the caller is famous simply because he or she is one of them. Who is this person? All the students are suspects. In order to find the culprit, everyone must be interviewed, their voices listened to carefully, until someone finds a speaker who sounds like the one on the tape.

In order to do this, the 'detectives' should talk to the 'suspects' [students will play each role, turn and turn about: see Game Plan (g)] and ask them questions which invite responses that could include the words and phrases of the station recording. The detectives should listen carefully to the sounds of the suspects' responses, possibly taping the answers. When the responses match the recording (when the dropping and adding of /h/, in the case of the suggested script, is matched) it sounds suspiciously like the burglar has been discovered . . .

Even if the 'detectives' are fairly sure, all along, which member of the group made the call to the station, they must still prove their suspicions through the careful questioning of a suspect followed by the careful description of his or her language and the matching of this with the recorded evidence. In this respect, they are in the same position as the police: suspicions alone are not sufficient grounds on which to make an arrest. (N.B. Comments in Game Plan, below, develop this broad outline of the Game.)

The Point of the Game

The Game provides a relatively simple and enjoyable opportunity to practise listening closely to the sounds of English and transcribing them, activities which students often find daunting.

At the very least, since this kind of investigation is undertaken in actual police work, the Game proves there can be real uses for phonetic transcription – something that students often find difficult to credit! [Older and more advanced students would find Baldwin and French (1990), a discussion of forensic phonetics, very interesting.] Of course, it has a wide range of applications. It can be used to describe and distinguish languages and language varieties, and is involved in speech therapy, language pathology and so on.

However, the Game might also begin a discussion of *phonology*, a consideration of the rule-governed way in which different languages arrange their *phonemes*. Phonemes are those sounds which, selected from the whole range of sounds the human vocal tract is able to make, are significant to meaning in a particular language. For English speakers, /p/ is significant and so is /b/, because we hear them as changing the meaning in words like 'pit' and 'bit'.

But not all languages hear the same set of sounds as meaningful. Moreover, not all languages accept the same organization of sounds. For instance, as Jean Aitchison (1987: 50) points out, if an English word begins with three consonant-type phonemes, the first of these will always be /s/, the second /p/, /t/ or /k/, and the third will be /l/, /r/, /w/ or /j/. The students might consider what could be produced if this rule was not followed. We should have words like *gwtl* or *brkpig* or *srvk*, and so on. Maybe these combinations crop up in some language, but not in English. All these issues, which the Game does no more than introduce, may be developed through, for example, Aitchison (1987), Ladefoged (1982) and Roach (1991).

The Game would also be a starting point for discussing regional, class and age differences in accent, for the sounds on the tape-recording would include clues to variables like gender, age and maybe region. Students may like to try another Game, **Sounds Familiar** (2.2), which explores attitudes to these variations of accent.

Afterword

Game plan

(a) This is not a particularly easy game. Unlike the majority of the others, it does involve some preparation – preparation that could take a little time and might be awkward to plan. The recording's script needs careful consideration [see (b) below]. And the class needs more directing and controlling than for other Games (otherwise they may spot the suspect before much practice in listening and using phonetic symbols has been achieved, though, even then, transcription will still be necessary for 'detectives' to prove their case).

(b) We incorporated a very specific feature in our recording. The student deliberately dropped every /h/ at the beginning of words, and added one in wherever possible. She therefore pronounced 'hurt' as 'urt' and 'ambulance' as 'hambulance'. Doing this meant the students had something easy to spot, transcribe and look out for in suspects – and ease of recognition is important if the Game's intention of dispelling anxiety about work of this kind is to be fulfilled. The particular feature we chose was not part of the recording student's normal speech. Therefore, the listening students were less likely to identify her too quickly.

(c) The students transcribe as a group but, to save time and anxiety, individual members can each take a different sentence from the script, asking for help from other team members where necesssary.

(d) In order to increase the investigative challenge (preventing the students from guessing the criminal before any transcription has been done), the first call could be slightly distorted – but only very slightly, of course, or it will be impossible to make a good transcript and a comparison with the suspect. We did this by using equipment which, on play-back, could slow the recording just a fraction. This tactic was sufficient to throw students off the scent, but not so far off that they could not, eventually, recognize the voice. Without this equipment, a similar minimal distortion could have been achieved if, on play-back, we had replaced good batteries with older ones.

(e) I was surprised to find that I had to help students think of questions to ask suspects in order to elicit responses that would be useful in relation to the added and subtracted /h/. We spent a few minutes planning possible questions (like 'What road is next to Outwoods Drive? Harrison Avenue or Hall Avenue?') before the interviews began.

(f) My group was a large one so, while everyone milled around playing either suspect or detective at the interview stage, I kept the students in their original transcribing teams in order to save time and confusion. Each team member took a turn as suspect, to be interviewed by the other three playing detectives. When one team thought they had found the culprit, they asked the rest of the class – before the suspect finally 'confessed' – to listen in and confirm their suspicions.

(g) The student who made our recording found it quite difficult to keep up the addition and subtraction of /h/ when she was being interviewed as a suspect. She did manage with a straight face, but I think it would have helped if I had practised an interview situation with her earlier. In order to keep the Game going enough to be profitable, we agreed beforehand that she would do her best to play detective first, suspect second.

International phonetic alphabet
related to key words for English vowels and consonants[a]

Vowels		Consonants	
/i/	beat	/p/	pin
/ɪ/	sit	/b/	bin
/ɛ/	get	/t/	tin
/æ/	bag	/d/	din
/ɑ/	calm	/k/	cool
/ɒ/	long	/g/	gale
/ɔ/	saw	/m/	many
/ɷ/	put	/n/	nose
/u/	moon	/ŋ/	si*ng*
/ʌ/	cup	/f/	fun
/ʒ/	bird	/v/	vat
/ə/	about	/θ/	*th*in
/eɪ/	day	/ð/	*th*at
/oɷ/	go	/s/	soap
/aɪ/	high	/z/	zip
/aɷ/	how	/ʃ/	shoe
/ɔɪ/	boy	/ʒ/	mea*s*ure
/ɪə/	here	/h/	hat
/ɛə/	there	/w/	weep
/ɔə/	four	/r/	red
/ɷə/	tour	/j/	yacht
		/l/	loose
		/tʃ/	*ch*eck
		/dʒ/	*j*ury

[a] The alphabet represents the initial sounds of these sample words except where indicated by italicization.

I am indebted to my colleague Elizabeth Morrish for preparing these lists.

Tutor and student comment

(a) I am very grateful to Terry Sylvester of The Nottingham Trent University Audio Visual Team for his help in making our recording.
(b) Some schools encountered difficulties with the Game but in other contexts its complicated preparation went smoothly, students found the play enjoyable, and it gave them confidence, later on, to try listening and transcribing in a more analytical and serious way.

1.7 SOUND SENSE

Sequel: **It's not what you say, but the way that you say it** . . .

Focus: Meaningful intonation and stress.

Age range: Junior to Higher Education.

Preparation time: Ten minutes to copy scripts before the role play.

Related Games: **Signing** (1.1), **Shaping Thought** (2.7).

The Game

The players divide into groups of four. All of the groups can play simultaneously. Two in each group are designated as 'field linguists' ready to observe what happens in the Game (as mentioned in Chapter 2, observers are always involved in the play). The other two should act out various roles in four different scenes. Those playing the scenes should have in front of them the short scripts given below. The observing linguists should not see these: they will then come to the language behaviour having no preconceived notions of what they are about to hear.

> *Scene One.* One student plays a minister saying 'Do you take this woman/ man to be your lawful wedded wife/husband?' The other plays a bride/ groom answering, 'I do'.
>
> *Scene Two.* A teacher says to a student, 'Who wants to get an A in the exam?' The student answers, 'I do'.
>
> *Scene Three.* A teacher says to a student, 'You never work hard in this class'. The student answers, 'I do!'
>
> *Scene Four.* One student says to another, 'You want to do language classes, don't you?' The other answers, 'I do?'

So long as the words 'I do' remain constant, other sentences in these brief exchanges may be altered to suit a particular group of students.

As one pair of students in each group plays out these scenes, the other two, working as linguists, should listen carefully to the contrasting sounds that mark each different utterance of 'I do'. The same actor should always play the 'I do' role, so these contrasts are not complicated by a change of voice, for the observing linguists are getting ready to describe – maybe to the whole class – the patterns of *intonation* and *stress* that they have heard. With the help of the acting pair, they can relate these different patterns to different meanings: to the meaning the actors intended to convey as they spoke, and the meaning the linguists thought they heard in their words.

The Point of the Game

The Game can offer two things:

(a) It draws attention to *intonation* and *stress*, two significant aspects of a language's 'phonology' (the way it selects from its available sound repertoire). That is, it pinpoints the sound effects that we add to the vowels and consonants – the *segments* – that make up words and sentences. Most importantly, it shows the potential of these *suprasegmental* features to *mean* over and above the sense of the words themselves [see also **Signing** (1.1)].

(b) It practises a specific descriptive linguistic skill, paving the way for analysis, which may be used again in other Games and in follow-ups like project work.

Intonation involves *pitch*, high or low. Pitch is made by the vibration of the vocal cords. The faster the vibration, the higher the pitch. Pitch moves. It can glide from high to low, low to high, producing a kind of tune.

When pitch is altered, or when a syllable is made louder or longer – or else these three variables are combined in some way – a sound comes over as *stressed*. Students will probably hear and, in their descriptions, refer to stress, and the rhythm it creates, as well as to change of 'tune' or intonation.

Intonation and stress play a significant part in meaning. In Scenes One, Two, Three and Four, the answering words remain the same: 'I do'. But their intonation and the contribution it makes, in conjunction with loudness or length of sound, to stress is different in every case. In consequence, each 'I do' carries a slightly different meaning. These differences relate here to *emotional*, *grammatical* or *informational* meaning. Suprasegmental elements of sound can also produce *indexical* meaning. (English is not, however, a *tone language* in the sense that a change in sound utterly alters the meaning of a word – as it does in over half the languages of the world. For example, in Mandarin Chinese, 'ma' can mean, depending on its tone, mother, hemp, horse or scold.)

Intonation and stress signal a difference of *grammatical* meaning between Scene Four and the others. It might be easiest to compare it with Scene Three.

Scene Four's intonation rises to indicate a question, and in the process 'do' sounds stressed. In Scene Three, the utterance will no doubt involve a falling tone (though it could rise first), expressing a statement.

Its sounds also add *emotional* meaning. The statement comes over as an exclamation, perhaps suggesting surprise, indignation or distress. As for Scene One, students might say that its answer, because of its tune and because of its balanced stress, sounds calm, definite. They might go further and conclude that such calm emotion indicates seriousness and commitment. Different descriptions and different interpretations of emotional meaning will be offered, depending on an actor's precise intonation and stress. Also, descriptions will vary slightly with the individual hearer. Teaching foreign students of English 'emotional' intonation is difficult for this reason. Native speakers know and more or less agree what different patterns mean – but the match between sound and sense is extremely subtle and learned through experience.

As for *informational* meaning, when pitch alters it can have significance through drawing our attention to a particular bit of speech: *I* do. Intonation could rise and fall, or fall and rise, on 'I', indicating that *I* want an A grade, never mind what the rest of the group wants! (see below for suggested descriptive notation). This emphasis is related to previous utterances, for we always draw attention to the 'new' bit of meaning, not the 'old' that has already been dealt with. In this case, the teacher's reference to an A grade assumes that somebody wants one: this is the given behind the response 'I do'. The fresh information in 'I do', is just precisely who wants one – '*I*'. 'Do' would not be emphasized here: no new information would be added if it were, and so the answer would sound odd, abnormal.

Stress and intonation can also add *indexical* meaning. That is, they can mark individual and group identity, for we may have personal intonational patterns or we may share those of different social or occupational groups, like auctioneers or army sergeants.

Students, even fairly young ones, will be able to describe informally the meaningful sound differences they hear, e.g. 'The words went up. She sounded cross'. But older students could go much further (perhaps using the Sequel below). They can be helped to describe the intonation they hear in terms of *tone units*, each with a *tone boundary*, and each unit having one *tone nucleus*, a point at which the tone moves. The boundaries (marked thus: / /) are sensed as a break or pause, sometimes infinitesimal. Students might use a simple notation, writing stressed syllables in capitals and describing with marks written above the words, a rising /i DÓ/, falling /i DÒ/, rise–fall /Î do/ or fall–rise /i DǑ/ shift in tone. As they formalize their descriptions, they may note more and more about the utterances and their sound patterns. Description and notation could then become more delicate, and Haynes (1989, ch. 11) would be helpful at this point.

Sequel

It's not what you say, but the way that you say it . . .

(a) After the initial game has been played and its Point explained, this can be reinforced and extended. Those older students who want to formalize their descriptions with the help of the notation mentioned above can work on a fifth scenario. This time they should pay particular attention to the 'teacher's' comment, and less attention to the 'I do' response:

> *Scene Five.* A teacher remarks, 'Here nobody words hard. You certainly don't'. The student player makes the usual response: 'I do'.

Different pairs of actors will probably interpret the teacher's utterance slightly differently. He or she may be drawing attention to 'here' or 'nobody' or 'hard': it depends upon what is the 'new' focus in the utterance and what it already 'given'. The teacher may be implying (meaning) anger, scorn, resignation, amusement. Therefore, the words he or she utters will be sounded – tuned and stressed – in a variety of ways. Tone nuclei will be placed differently, different syllables made louder or longer.

These differences can be discussed between the groups, their contrasts described in some detail and intuitions about their implications carefully assessed.

(b) Students can practise making their own intonation and stress as meaningful as possible. Try taking some basic text like a weather forecast, football results, even a page from the phone book, and reading it out:

 (i) indicating anger, joy, surprise (using intonation and stress to express emotional meaning);
(ii) as a preacher, auctioneer, sergeant-major (using intonation and stress indexically to express group identity).

Alternatively, they might decide on the typical sound patterns of, say, football results or weather forecasts and use these patterns with words from a totally different kind of context – knitting pattern language, say – asking listeners to guess where the sound model is normally used.

Afterword

Game plan

(a) The given sentences for the five Scenes, and the texts used for the Sequel, can of course be varied to suit the age and interest of the players. Delicacy of description can increase with the age and expertise of the players, but quite simple observations about changes in sound will make the Game's basic Point.
(b) Throughout the Game, the 'actors' can help the 'linguists' in their job of

describing the utterances and their possible meanings. But they will not be able to concentrate on this task. So, especially if the Sequel is played, it may be helpful for the two pairs within each group of four to widen their experience by exchanging roles: the actors become linguists and vice versa.

Tutor and student comment

(a) The game is relatively easy to set up, I have encountered no pitfalls, and students seem satisfied because they can quickly do a lot with a small amount of material.
(b) Players said they liked working with the brief utterance, 'I do'. Its brevity helped them to recall it – and thence the linguistic Point of the Game. Besides, they found being able to vary so short a sentence in so many ways emphasized the very considerable power of intonation and stress.

1.8 LANGUAGE FOR LIVING

Sequel: **The metaphors of AIDS**

Focus: Our everyday use of metaphor and its effect on our thinking.

Age range: The Game's Point is complex and therefore players probably need to be at least GCSE level and perhaps sixth-form in order to take after-play discussion very far.

Preparation time: Kind Edward VII Community College suggests it would be useful to develop the background given in the Point of the Game, so it could be helpful if staff looked at Lakoff and Johnson's (1980) *Metaphors We Live By* before the Game. If the Sequel is used, staff and students will need to read Susan Sontag's (1989) essay, *AIDS and Its Metaphors*, first.

Related Games: **Shaping Thought** (2.7) extends the Point of this Game with discussion of the Whorfian hypothesis (referred to very briefly in this Game).

The Game

The Game is in two stages:

Stage One
First, the whole class should think about how we all use metaphors to talk about everyday experiences. For example, as Lakoff and Johnson (1980) demonstrate in their book *Metaphors We Live By*, we may talk about time as if it were money (*well spent, wasted, saved*). We might refer, metaphorically, to arguments as though they were battles (*I won that one because her arguments completely misfired* or *The opposing team got shot down in flames*). And love is often spoken of as if it were madness (*They were crazy about each other*) or

perhaps as a matter of health (*They're love-sick* or *That relationship is on the mend*).

Next, groups of about half a dozen students (working simultaneously) should each tell a story. This might be done by the first storyteller making up an introductory bit – perhaps just a sentence – and the next person picking up where he or she leaves off, and so on, inventing round the group.

There are just two rules for the storytelling. Firstly, the tale must centre on a relationship in which there is an argument about the time a couple have together. Secondly, the argument, the time and the relationship should be talked about, wherever appropriate, through their everyday metaphors of money, battle and sickness or madness. A sample story might read something like:

> Jack was *crazy* about Jill. But he played football. She kept *sniping* at him, grumbling that he didn't *spend* enough time with her. Jill *fired* accusation after accusation at him, but *called a truce* when Jack reminded her that she went swimming every Wednesday – a complete *waste of time*, in his opinion.

As the storytelling progresses, students should be thinking about how difficult, or how easy, it is to use these metaphors.

Stage Two
Next, the whole class should suggest alternative and unusual metaphors for time, for argument and for relationships. For example, time might be thought of as food, a relationship as a piece of music, argument as a dance for couples, and so on. The argument-as-dance metaphor might go as follows:

> They started off apart, but then they began moving step by step, closely together. He whirled her along with him and, in the end, though she executed a few solo glissades, they came to rest at exactly the same point.

Yet another story should now be told, again about a couple's argument over time, but now using these alternative, odd, not to say bizarre metaphors – or, better still, choosing equally unusual ones suggested, prior to this second round of storytelling, by the class. Each group should either include an observer, taking note of how the metaphors are used or, if it will not inhibit the students, the telling should be tape-recorded for discussion later.

As they tell the tale, the students should be wondering about the appropriateness of such unusual metaphors: Are they ridiculously inept – or are they in some way thought-provoking, revealing a fresh angle on life? Do we find new ways of seeing as we experiment with new language?

The Point of the Game
'Metaphoring' involves, of course, talking about A in terms of B. Someone may say, 'That man (A) is a lion (B)'. Naturally, the sentence cannot be

literally true: it is a contradiction in terms. But it may still, in a sense, be correct. That is, it may be *experientially* true. If this particular man has, in the experience of the speaker, some lion-like qualities, then in a way he or she is making an accurate statement. Perhaps the man is, in the speaker's view, particularly brave, strong, noble, heroic – or dangerous. If so, when B qualities of this kind reflect back on A, the assertion is true and revealing.

As Lakoff and Johnson point out, we 'live' by such metaphors: they are not restricted to the imaginative language of literature, they also belong to everyday talk. This should be proved by Stage One of the Game. Telling a tale of love, time and argument through metaphors of sickness, madness, money and war is unlikely to be difficult. In fact, it is probably impossible to make up the story without them because, for us in our culture, such metaphors are experientially true. It is appropriate enough – experientially true enough – given our culture's kind of economy to talk of time as money. For we earn money per hour, week, month's effort. If we do not work for a period of time, we do not earn money. Then again, in our experience, those in love may behave as if they are unwell or unstable. And arguments often seem like what we know of pitched battles.

On the other hand, we are not accustomed to thinking of argument in the way that Stage Two of the Game suggests, as a cooperative venture like a dance which, carefully executed, can reach a mutually satisfactory conclusion. The implications of this particular metaphor are so unlike our actual experience that using it may seem ridiculous. In this case, it cannot be one to live by.

Yet, although the metaphors we do live by must seem experientially true, they do not necessarily tell the whole truth and nothing but the truth. For while they put the spotlight on one aspect of an experience, they may also hide – leave in shadow – other potential parts of that experience. Indeed, students might wonder if we 'live by metaphors' to such a high degree that our customary language actually discourages us from perceiving every angle on our world.

Does our customary language about spending time, for instance, blind us to a more leisured use of it? Does it contribute to feelings of guilt whenever we are not using it 'economically'? It may well do. (Incidentally, an item on the news recently concerned a firm which is presently fining its over-working employees if they do *not* take their holiday allocation!)

If we do feel guilt about 'wasted' time, what happens if we speak of time in a different way? What if we used language, as Stage Two of the Game suggests, associated with a good meal? Would we then try to 'savour' time, maybe 'flavour' it to our taste with carefully chosen activities, and so on? *Could* we see it this way, would there be any experiential truth in the perception?

As for love, if we experimented with 'languaging' it as a piece of music, to be composed with harmony, some discord, careful attention to tradition balanced with judicious innovation, and also a consideration for audience and the cost of performance, would we be helped to view our relationships from a different angle? Would we then conduct them any differently?

These questions raise another, fundamental one: Which comes first, the chicken or the egg – language or experience? Discussion of this final question will also provide a suitable lead into the Games and activities of Stage Two and of course relates particularly to the Whorfian hypothesis which is part of the Point of the Game, **Shaping Thought** (2.7).

However, staff might like to raise the Whorfian hypothesis here, explaining to students the arguments of the American linguist and anthropologist, Edward Sapir (1884–1936), and his student, Benjamin Lee Whorf (1897–1941), who suggested that we see the world through our particular language. The strongest version of the hypothesis implies that our particular language *determines* the way we think and, since different people speak different languages, our thinking about our world is necessarily *relatively* different. A weaker version of the hypothesis suggests that language does not so much determine as *encourage* our thinking.

Sequel

The metaphors of AIDS

Older students might like to go on, from the Game and its immediate Point, to read and discuss Susan Sontag's (1989) essay *AIDS and Its Metaphors*. Sontag argues that the language we habitually choose to talk about AIDS – seeing it, for example, as 'plague' and languaging public response to it as 'war' – blinds us to the whole truth about the disease and in this way contributes to inaccurate, distressing and dangerous misunderstanding. If this is so, we could say, picking up on the Lakoff and Johnson theme, that the metaphors of AIDS are not ones to live by – but to die by. The metaphor of plague, for instance, may carry with it implications that the disease comes as a punishment and moral judgement. The notion of war regards the disease as an enemy and may therefore legitimize any means used to attack it: it could even imply that those who suffer from the disease are themselves the enemy.

So, what do the students think? Could these metaphors be abandoned, as Sontag urges? How might they be replaced? How have they arisen? (see also Shepherd, forthcoming, *Literature about Language*).

Afterword

Game plan

(a) If students need encouragement to use metaphors in either story, the groups can be in competition with each other, team points being awarded every time an appropriate metaphor is used. In this case, each storytelling group should include an observing scorekeeper.

(b) I wrote metaphors on the board – both the conventional for Stage One and the unconventional for Stage Two – as students thought of them in our preliminary discussion. I left these lists up, thinking they would prompt the tale telling. But the groups felt the ready-made supply of ideas took a bit of spontaneous creativity out of the game. Certainly, if conventional metaphors are truly waiting on the tips of our tongues, then we should not need lists to remind us of them. But perhaps the lists are useful prompts for the second round of tale telling.

(c) Tupton Hall School found it helped students to start their second round of tales if staff had first given them an example of a story told with 'odd' metaphors.

(d) Either a time limit or a specific number of turns (say, twice round the group) should be set for the storytelling, otherwise metaphors begin to be repeated and the Game can pall.

Tutor and student comment

(a) Tupton Hall School students found this stimulating and productive. They followed it with discussion of the Whorfian hypothesis. (In particular, they discussed the degree to which the language of colour categorizes reality, some cultures choosing to label many more shades of the spectrum than others: see Berlin and Kay 1969.)

(b) Charles Keene College found that Stage One played well. However, Stage Two was harder because the groups, playing with my suggested new metaphors, did not view the world in the ways these suggest. Of course, this difficulty helps to make the Game's Point, and Charles Keene staff found discussion opened out well.

(c) This Game can be incredibly noisy! If it is played by competitive teams, the excitement mounts – but then, so does productive enthusiasm. It is extremely easy to set up, usually makes its Point quite clearly, and can lead on to a lot of (quieter) class discussion.

(d) Students thought my suggestion of musical composition, as a metaphor for love, was unoriginal. They reminded me that we already talk of harmonious couples, of relationships out of sync and so on. Instead they suggested a fairground metaphor might be more useful: coconut shies, merry-go-rounds, all the fun of the fair and so on! Still, I think that taking the music metaphor a good bit further, as I outline above – beyond ideas of harmony and synchronization – is still out of the ordinary and thought-provoking. For instance:

> I'm afraid the Smiths are writing their marriage with the in-laws in mind: both sets of parents are very knowledgeable critics – marriage-buffs in front-row seats for every new composition in the family.

Still, their honeymoon was the perfect overture: it contained all the elements of their life to come – passion, tenderness, repetition and the occasional discord.

SECTION 2
LANGUAGE IN PERFORMANCE

Spoken language

2.1 VARIETY PERFORMANCE

Sequel: **What's my line?**

Focus: The study of register, the interrelationship of language and situation, with a critical look at the notion of 'appropriateness'.

Age range: Providing that suitable scenarios are used, the Game can be played at any age.

Preparation time: Nil.

Related Games: **Sounds Familiar (2.2), Talking Power (2.3), Cross Talk (2.4), Talking 'Proper'? (2.6).**

The Game

(a) *Participants.* The players should divide into groups of four. Two members of each group are to act as observer linguists. One of the others should play himself or herself as a student. The fourth member should take on a variety of roles in succession: first, the Head of the student's school or college; second, the student's close friend; third, one of the student's parents or a close relative.

(b) *Situation.* A situation should be chosen bearing in mind the age of the players. Young ones might imagine that the pupil in the Game is feeling unwell at the prospect of a disliked lesson and wants to be excused the class. The pupil explains the situation, in turn, to the Head, the friend and the relative. Older students might imagine they have to tell these three people that, after all, they do not want to sit A Level examinations. There are a number of possibilities so long as the imagined event involves the student player in conveying a 'sensitive' message. If these mini-dramas can be recorded on tape, so much the better.

(c) *Follow-up.* The pairs of observing students will (following suggestions made below) describe to their own small groups – and then, probably, to the class as a whole – the kind of language they have heard. In each of the three scenarios it will be different. Together with the role-playing students, these observers will analyse and explain the chosen language, relating its choices (see Point of the Game) to the situation and its participants. Analyses will be facilitated if tape-recordings have been made for students to reflect upon the scenes.

The Point of the Game

This is a relatively simple and easy Game to play, with very general, but important, objectives:

• introducing the concept of language variation in relation to situation;
• practising linguistic skills of description, analysis and critical explanation;
• considering the concept of 'appropriate' language.

Variety Performance will therefore act as a convenient ice breaker and as an introduction to the more precisely focused Games that follow in this second Section.

As the Game will demonstrate, we vary the way we use language, 'styling' it [see **Shaping Thought** (2.7) and **Form and Focus** (2.8)] by choosing from its available 'systems' of sounds, words and syntax (those elements of our linguistic competence played with in Section 1 of the Games). The situation we find ourselves in leads us to do so: the study of *register* is concerned with variety of language in relation to context. Involved in register are what Halliday calls field, tenor and mode (see Morley 1985: 47–8):

• *Mode* refers to the medium of the text, spoken or written. Of course, there could be further categories. A news bulletin, for instance, is written but with the intention of speaking it.
• The *field* is the subject being spoken or written about. It also refers to the people, things or events involved, and the time and place of their happening.
• *Tenor* is concerned with the personalities, social roles and status of the people involved, so it refers to matters like formality and technicality. It also includes reference to the function of the language used – whether or not it is, for instance, asking, directing or describing.

Section 1 of the Games played with the elements of language from which we can choose in the situations we encounter. In Chomsky's terms, we put these elements of our linguistic 'competence' [discussed in **Knowing the Rules** (1.3)] into 'performance', in real situations. But Chomsky concentrates his work on competence, leaving performance to other linguists (not all of whom believe such a sharp distinction can be made between the two aspects of language). One of these, Hymes (1971), suggests that as we acquire language we also achieve 'communicative competence': we learn to use language in the way our culture/society/family/peer group, and so on, expects. We might say that we know, more or less, how to choose from our language options *appropriately* (but see below) in a given situation.

However, it is not precisely the linguist's job to say how language *should* be used in a particular situation: it is not the job of the linguist to be *prescriptive*. On the contrary, in the first instance, the linguist's work is *descriptive*. He or she will need to observe closely the language heard or read, paying attention to such features as syntax, phonology and vocabulary. Those observing the Game will practise this descriptive skill. They might ask themselves the following kinds of questions, using in their answers the knowledge and metalanguage acquired in the Section 1 Games.

1 Does the person playing the student role use different *words* when speaking to the Head, the friend and the relative? If so, how do they differ?
2 Does this player's *tone of voice* (including its intonation and its paralinguistic features) alter? In what ways?
3 Does the *pace* or *rhythm* of the language alter? How?
4 Does the *length of sentences* vary? How?
5 Does the *syntax* seem different in any way? How?
6 Was there a change of *accent*? What kind of change?
7 Were any *other significant language differences* noted?

Observers might also describe the mini-dramas following Hymes's 'SPEAK-ING' approach, discussed in **Cross Talk** (2.4).

Older students may raise the possibility that the classroom context and the presence of observers, could – as well as the imagined scenarios – be affecting the language choices in the game. If so, this will provide an opportunity to consider some methodological difficulties in sociolinguistic investigation, particularly the so-called 'observer's paradox'. These are discussed in Wardaugh (1986: 145–57) (the issue will be raised again, in more detail, in Chapter 4).

After description, the professional linguist can personally take his or her work further, or pass on the descriptions that have been made to a colleague who has whatever specialist knowledge is needed for analysis and explanation. A psycholinguist, for instance, could use descriptions of children's language in work on the acquisition of language. The careful description of language can also form the starting point for literary criticism. And the Games which follow in this second Section of Chapter 3 all start from the careful observation of aspects of language before going on to analyse and explain speech or writing in social contexts – as far as possible, given the students' age and experience and perhaps aided by knowledge acquired from other parts of the curriculum (as discussed in Chapters 1 and 2).

One of the issues students might debate in their explanation is the very notion of 'appropriateness' and communicative 'competence'. What, exactly, is appropriateness? Who decides what is, or is not, competent? And where do linguists fit in, especially since their role is not 'prescriptive'?

First, these standards of 'appropriateness' are not exactly like the rules of (Chomskyan) competence, the rules of the systems of language. For one thing, although it needs a language-using environment to flourish, competence seems [as we discussed in **Knowing the Rules** (1.3)] to be based on something that is innate: the communicative competence of performance, on the other hand, appears to be more culturally and socially shaped. Then, we can break the conventions of appropriateness and still be understood: we could, for example, deliver a monologue when normally a more equally distributed conversational exchange might have been expected, yet we cannot start jumbling up the usual English word order without distorting our intended message. But some situations are more socially circumscribed than others. So, whilst we might possibly choose rude language behaviour in conversation with our head teacher, we are less likely to demand that a barrister answers our questions, since it is the norm that barristers in court ask and we answer.

But who decrees such norms? Not, as already noted, the linguist: the linguist is not a privileged instigator or guardian of language behaviour, merely an observer. Yet, as in any profession, observers can be *critical*, wondering as they attempt to explain the language behaviour they have carefully described and analysed, why the conventions have become established and what their effects are upon those who use the language behaviour that is considered appropriate to such norms.

It would clearly be silly for an expert in cookery to speak on television about a recipe as if he or she were standing on the terraces shouting encouragement to a football team: it would be 'inappropriate' for reasons (why?) that do not seem contentious. But, the linguist might look [as we do in **Talking Power** (2.3)] at the conventional communicative competence of men and women and of powerful and powerless people, considering where their habits of language may have come from and what the effects of these are. Do they, in the light of this consideration, seem 'appropriate', or could they and should they be changed? A linguist might also [as players do in **Sounds Familiar** (2.2) and in **Talking 'Proper'?** (2.6)] look at the conventional use of Standard and Non-standard forms of English: Who chooses which, why, when, to what effect?

Older students, wishing to develop their critical explanation, would be interested in work by critical linguists such as Hodge, Kress or Fairclough – always remembering of course that attitudes to language and to language users are, as we noted in Chapter 1 and discussed in **Sounds Familiar** (2.2), very strong and very deep in all of us. Even the critical linguist, as those in the 'critical' school themselves point out, is not exempt from, and has to take account of, the subtle pressures of ideology and personal bias.

Sequel

What's my line? (or, who, what, and where am I?)
We can recognize sets of vocabulary, and ways of saying, that relate to particular occupations or to very clearly defined social groups. For instance, there is the language of medicine as used in the GP's surgery, the language of the Church as delivered from the pulpit, the language of air traffic control spoken to a pilot in the air, the language of music enthusiasts at a concert, the language of football supporters at a match, and so on. Students could therefore play a version of the old television game 'What's My Line?' Instead of indicating their occupation or special interest with a mime, a player should deliver to the class a short monologue in the 'appropriate' language (bearing in mind field, tenor and mode). Scripts for these might be worked out in pairs, the students pooling their knowledge of the kinds of language that are typical. Points could then be awarded to the listener who first identifies the correct 'who, what, where', and most importantly, can *describe the features of language* which were significant clues. No doubt observers would spot, say, the language of a tennis commentator at Wimbledon without any difficulty at all, but they must also be able to say that, for instance, the vocabulary is specialized, with words like 'love', 'advantage' and 'set' having meanings peculiar to context.

Afterword

Tutor and student comment
Students have no difficulty recognizing that language does vary, but describing its distinctions is a challenge. However, it is a challenge that is comfortably met in the context of playing the Game. Those who, nevertheless, might still be asking 'why bother to describe a variety I know exists even without close scrutiny?', may be assured that descriptive skills will be used later on in, say, Games relating to gender or advertising or cultural difference, and are essential if anything substantial is to be said about the power of language in these significant contexts.

2.2 SOUNDS FAMILIAR

Sequel: **Non-standard words and syntax**

Focus: Attitudes to language varieties and to their users.

Age range: From 11 years to Higher Education.

Preparation time: Pre-taped/video-taped advertisements may be used, but this is not absolutely essential.

Related Games: **Variety Performance** (2.1), **Talking 'Proper'?** (2.6).

The Game

The Game is in two Stages. Stage One can stand alone. It is preferable to discuss the Point of the Game before beginning Stage Two.

Stage One

(a) The whole class might first watch a selection of video-taped TV commercials, or listen to tape-recorded radio adverts. Alternatively, if it is not convenient to actually watch or listen to the advertisements, students can be asked to recall any that especially interest them.

(b) As they watch or describe their recollections, the students should take note of the varying accents used by the actors in the adverts. Do they identify them as British or foreign? Do they sound, say, French, Italian, Japanese, American, English, Scottish, Welsh, Irish? Can the students be even more precise about where the accents come from? For instance, if the voices have a Scottish ring, do they sound Glaswegian? Or does the accent suggest Edinburgh? If the voices seem to come from England, are they from the North or the South? Do they seem to belong to the country or the city? Which place exactly? Do the speakers sound young or old? Are their voices upper class, middle class or working class? The students should record their answers.

(c) Now the players should ask themselves the following questions about each of the voices in turn. Their answers should be as spontaneous as possible.

   (i) Do they like or dislike the voice?
   (ii) Does the voice make them laugh?
   (iii) Does the voice make them feel reassured?
   (iv) Does the voice suggest its user is intelligent?
   (v) Does the voice suggest its user is attractive?
   (vi) Does the voice suggest anything particular not mentioned in (i–v)?

(d) Next, the students should wonder why a particular voice is used in a particular advert: Why might it be relevant? In what ways could it encourage the hearer to respond positively to the product for sale? For example, if the 'natural' qualities of a product – perhaps a particular kind of bread or honey – are its selling point, do rural sounding voices on the commercial somehow help to emphasize this feature and make it attractive? Is so, why? Does the bank manager in a finance advert have a 'posh' voice or not? Why? What kinds of voices do his or her clients have? Why? Might the viewer want to use the bank in question more (or less) if the client's voice sounded like the bank manager's? There are no clearly right or wrong answers to these questions. What counts, for the purposes of the Game, is eliciting the players' instinctive feelings on such matters, since these will be influenced by their own *attitudes* to language.

The students' discussions so far (b and c above) will help this debate (d), but their thinking will probably be more fruitful if the Point of the Game is explained now, before going on to Stage Two. Besides, if Stage Two were to be played first, before discussion of the Point, it could merely reinforce, rather than critically consider (part of the Point), students' own existing attitudes.

The Point of the Game

If we find ourselves among strangers, we begin at once to 'place' them. We wonder, perhaps unconsciously, what their social background is, where they come from, maybe what they do for a living. To answer our queries we shall find clues in their general demeanour, their dress, what they say to us – and, most importantly for this Game, *how* they say it. If a new acquaintance speaking English comes from abroad, then his or her accent will very likely tell us so, but we may be unable to glean much more from the voice. If, on the other hand, the speaker is from Britain and so are we, then we shall probably be able to place this person, through his or her voice, more accurately. If the speaker is actually from our own part of the British Isles, then we may be very specific indeed, identifying the person's home town, maybe even the exact area in this town. For, without necessarily being aware of it, as we acquire language we also come to equate certain things with certain kinds of accent.

The way a voice sounds can be an indication of the speaker's class. The Standard, or 'RP' sound ('received pronunciation' as it is called, 'received' implying 'generally accepted' as in 'received wisdom') – the so-called 'posh' accent – may suggest to the hearer that its user is middle or upper class. If it is Non-standard, it may 'mean', to the hearer, lower class. Or it can indicate the region the speaker comes from. (RP is not a regional marker, of course. It is heard everywhere.) Incidentally, some members of the Royal Family do not use RP. Being upper-upper class, as it were, they have an accent – a 'hyperlect' – all of their own. There is a kind of spectrum of accents, from the basilect, through the mesolect, the acrolect and the hyperlect. Honey (1989: 54) explains:

> The term ACROLECT describes the dialect (or accent) which is accorded highest prestige: in British English the accent concerned in this category is . . . RP. The 'broadest' form of popular speech is called the BASILECT. In 1850, the majority of people in rural areas, especially those with least education, spoke a basilect: those forms survive now among 'elderly people with little education' (as one scholar puts it) in rather isolated areas. With every year that passes, fewer and fewer young children are introduced to the meanings of the old dialect words, and the accents of more of them move to at least an intermediate stage in the direction of RP, which is called the MESOLECT . . . the special form of RP associated with the very highest category of social privilege . . . [is the] HYPERLECT.

[Note that, as we shall make clear again in **Talking 'Proper'?** (2.6), 'dialect' refers to word and syntax choices as well as to sound, whereas 'accent' refers only to sound.]

But generalizations about class and region are not the only responses we may make to accent. Studies (see Honey 1989, ch. 4) have shown that people equate the RP accent with intelligence, authority, capability and so on. A Non-RP accent, associated with a particular region or with a lower class, suggests to some listeners a less intelligent, less able person. Astonishingly, even those who use non-RP accents themselves often make these pejorative judgements (Honey 1989: 53–4). So why does anyone choose to retain a non-RP accent? Well, many people believe that a non-RP accent means the speaker is friendly, warm, an attractive person with a sense of humour. Besides, if your peers use non-RP, but you sound different, you may find yourself excluded from their circle.

Is it reasonable to make such broad value judgements on the basis of sound? Do the students agree on a clear image of personality that they always associate with a 'Brummy' or with a 'Scouse' accent? If so, can it be fair – or logical – to assume that *all* Birmingham and Liverpool people with these accents have these stereotypical personalities? Besides, if our accent is not RP, why should hearers assume they know, from our voice, something about our intelligence? After all, the way a version of English sounds rarely makes it any less communicative than any other. Derek Jameson, the successful Fleet Street editor turned highly articulate broadcaster, with distinctive non-RP accent, surely makes this point. And, conversely, why, if we *do* speak RP, should we sometimes be rejected by those who do not, apparently on the assumption that we are different in unacceptable ways?

Of course, as the Game makes clear, it is true that accents do signal *something*. If we are born and bred in Manchester we are not likely to have a Lincolnshire sound. If our family is of a higher social class, we are more likely to use RP than non-RP. But, if listened to carefully, accents signify not merely broad, generalized group stereotypes – with questionable accuracy – but also individuals, separate personalities. They signal *us*. Our voices are ourselves, speaking for us as individuals, as well as members of a family and of class and regional groups, and so on. So each of us has a slightly different voice (as the John Donne Radio 2 game, in which listeners are asked to guess a person's identity simply from his or her voice, goes to prove). It is not surprising, then, that the Kingman Report and subsequent language teaching initiatives have recognized that 'speakers may be rightly proud of their regional pronunciation' (Kingman 1988: 14) and make no attempt to eradicate it from speech.

But still the stereotypes are potent. We open our mouths and we may talk ourselves into – or out of – a friendship or a job. First impressions count, however unfairly. And television/radio itself feeds on – and fosters – this kind of stereotypical response.

Remember the common value judgement, mentioned above, that people using non-RP accents are warm, lively, humorous, friendly? Now, take an advert (shown in 1990) for a certain canned lager – not the kind of drink conventionally served at an elegant dinner table, more the sort associated with a macho and workaday image. Viewers saw it being drunk by a group of tough-looking youths, joking in a non-RP accent. The butt of their joke was an RP-speaking, older couple. These two completely misunderstood what was being said to them – because it was said in an accent not their own – and consequently looked foolish and rather twee. The lads called for another round to celebrate their one-upmanship . . .

In sorting out the implications and likely effects of advertisements such as this one, students will be focusing on feelings, value judgements and pre-judices towards accents of region and class. They will not only be theorizing about other people's strong reactions but, equally importantly, they will be recognizing their *own* attitudes to such matters and measuring the depth and strength of their feelings – they will be doing the kind of critical linguistics discussed in Chapters 1 and 2 and referred to in **Variety Performance** (2.1).

So now is a good time to go on to Stage Two of the Game. If it had been played before the Point was discussed, it might have been dictated by attitudes that had not been thought through. Attitudes must still influence the Game – that is its Point – but now they will be considered and their full force more consciously understood.

Stage Two
The students should divide up into small groups. Now, in the light of their observations about the commercials (i.e. the students' placing of accents ac-cording to country, region, class and so on, their attitudes to these accents, and their assessment of the appropriateness of each voice for each advert) each group should choose a product and write an original script to advertise it – deciding carefully on the accents involved (for an alternative procedure, see the Game Plan, below).

If the Point of the Game has been explained before they begin to draft their scripts, the students will be conscious of the strong attitudes viewers (and advertisers themselves) can hold towards accents and choose their media voices accordingly and critically. It is a complex issue, for whilst students may not wish to reinforce a biased attitude they must, as advertisers, sell their products.

Finally, the groups should explain to the class as a whole why they have chosen a particular voice for a particular commercial. If they are confident enough to act out their script – with designated accents of course! – so much the better.

Sequel

Non-standard words and syntax
The Game has concentrated on accent, but of course accent is only one distin-guishing feature of talk. Our words and grammar may also place us as three activities that follow here emphasize.

True, many of us, while favouring a Non-standard accent, still use Standard syntax and lexicon. But we may, on the other hand, use Non-standard words and grammar, or just Non-standard words, as well as non-RP accent, and whilst the Kingman Report argues that all children have a 'right' to learn Standard English, it also insists that this should be *added* to repertoires. It should not replace a Non-standard variety which is an additional 'source of richness' (Kingman 1988: 14).

(a) For example, some of us call a narrow way an 'alley', but people from Dorset may say 'drong' and those from Nottingham may choose 'ginnel'. Students could make lists of comparative terms.

As for Non-standard forms of grammar, these are less heard in contexts of power and prestige, and they are discouraged (the Kingman Report insists this should be so) in writing. But they are no less complex and structured – and above all no less expressive – than the model that, for historical reasons, is now regarded as Standard.

(b) So students might read William Barnes's Dorset poetry (Jones 1962), or Alfred Tennyson's poems in Lincolnshire dialect (Ricks 1969), or Tom Leonard's work in Glaswegian (1984) and also his own thinking on dialect writing (1987) (see also Shepherd 1990).

(c) They might listen to a West Indian selecting a variety of syntax from those available along the continuum from an English-based Creole to Standard English. If any of the students has this range available to them personally, it would be helpful if they would draw attention to the differences.

Afterword

Game plan

(a) As regards making the Game's Point, simply recalling adverts is probably just as satisfactory as watching or listening to them in class. But clearly, using the recordings of the actual commercials adds another dimension to the Game.

(b) It is not essential for players to write out the whole of their own, original script. They can describe the advert they envisage in general terms, making clear the kinds of voices they would cast and why.

(c) Stage One of the Game, in association with the Point of the Game, could stand alone as the nucleus of a class.

Tutor and student comment

(a) There is no problem getting students to recall adverts they have seen, or to invent fresh scripts. Charles Keene College found the Game an enjoyable approach to the topic. It works well in that it provokes lively discussion.

(b) Most importantly, players were well aware that *other* people make value judgements about accents, and there was general agreement about what these judgements might be. But frequently players were amazed at the strength of their own feelings about different voices: there was often a clash between their conscious intellectual responses and their underlying feelings and beliefs.

2.3 TALKING POWER

Sequel: **Boys, girls and oral exams**

Focus: Language and its variation in relation to gender.

Age range: From 14 years to Higher Education.

Preparation time: A few minutes to prepare and photocopy lists of the linguistic features that are to be listened for.

Related Games: **Variety Performance** (2.1), **Cross Talk** (2.4), **Winning words** [Sequel to **Cracking the Joke!** (2.5)], **Shaping Thought** (2.7).

The Game

The Game is based on a role play around the following information.

(a) *Imagined venue.* The Head of School/College's office.
(b) *Time.* Following some crucial examinations.
(c) *Players.* The Head, a fairly new teacher, a student, and one of the student's parents. The gender of these participants should be decided upon by the players.
(d) *Background.* The student has been given a fail grade for one of his or her papers. This has serious consequences. If it is an Advanced Level mock that has been failed, there are implications for the grades to be predicted on college application forms. If it was a first-year GCSE exam, the student might not be allowed to proceed with the subject to the second year [see Game Plan (a), p. 85]. The student claims to have had an asthmatic attack on the Saturday and Sunday before the Monday exam and therefore could not revise. A doctor was not called because the asthmatic tendency is chronic and the necessary medicines were in the house; besides, it was the weekend and only an emergency surgery was held. The student could not see the doctor on the Monday morning – when traces of the asthma were still noticeable – because he or she was sitting the paper. However, the student claims that the remains of the asthma, plus lack of revision due to the attack, led to the disastrous performance. The staff say the paper was failed because the student was too lazy to prepare and the illness is not proven.
(e) *The Scene.* A meeting is about to take place. It has been asked for by the student to ask for the fail grade to be reconsidered on grounds of impaired performance.

(f) *The Audience*. The audience should act as linguistic researchers, carefully noting and describing how the language works. It would be useful for these observers to have in front of them a checklist of what to listen for. For instance:

- Who talks most?
- Who interrupts?
- Who is interrupted?
- Who seems most polite?
- Who encourages whom?

Each 'researcher' could choose one of the four players to concentrate upon. Alternatively, the researchers could each listen out for a different language feature. The latter strategy seems to work particularly well.

If a class on language and gender has taken place before the Game, there could be more specific features of language behaviour (listed immediately below) to observe. Or it could be re-played with these in mind, after the Point has been discussed. Such features would include:

- overlaps as distinct from interruptions;
- hedges;
- the presence or absence of minimal responses;
- tag questions of either the 'undercutting' or the facilitating kind.

These are defined in the Point of the Game. However, if the actors have been included in discussion of such features, it is possible they will self-consciously modify their talk accordingly. In our experience, though, this has not happened (which suggests that habits and expectations of these aspects of communicative competence are deeply ingrained).

The Point of the Game

The Game practises skills of observation and description and encourages critical evaluation of the linguistic relationship of men and women. A popular impression is that we can define a 'male' language and a contrasting 'female' language – a female language that is in some ways disadvantaged by the male. This disadvantage is usually identified in the lexicon: there seem to be more English words that are prejudicial to women than to men (for example, the often quoted 'master/mistress' contrast). However, it must be remembered that words are empty carcases [see Point of the Game, especially in relation to the Whorfian hypothesis, in **Shaping Thought** (2.7)]. They are nothing without their human users to breathe life into them: master and mistress are complementary or insulting depending entirely upon the intention of their speaker and the inclination of their hearer. It is *use* of language that is crucial to its meaning and impact. In this Game, therefore, we concentrate not so much on the choice of words, but experiment with words and syntax in action between the sexes. Significant features of this discourse are italicized in the discussion which follows.

Men appear – in some recent experiments – to take the conversational advantage. In mixed groups they tend to *choose the topic* for discussion and then speak more than women, keen to deliver long *monologues* at the slightest excuse. Moreover, they *interrupt* women, cutting into the middle of their talk and, in this way, taking away their conversational turn, effectively silencing them. Men in these studies do not, however, interrupt each other very much. Women also avoid interrupting men – and members of their own sex. They do occasionally *overlap*. That is, rather than taking the liberty of stopping a speaker's talk mid-stream, they may just 'clip' the end of their utterance – but they are more likely to overlap women than men.

So it would seem, according to such studies (e.g. Zimmerman and West, Swacker, Holmes, Brouer – see Coates 1986), that women do not prevent men having their conversational way. In fact, they may actually encourage them by asking of men, more than of other women, *questions* which invite lengthy response. They then stay almost silent themselves – but occasionally make encouraging *minimal responses*, murmuring to the male speaker 'mhm, surely, right, yes, go on'. Men apparently deny those women who do manage to get a word in edgeways the assistance of such helpful minimal responses.

Frustrated and discouraged by this kind of denial, women may resort to asking men *tag questions*. These, 'tagged' to the end of one of their statements, do demand some kind of response: 'It's my evening too, *isn't it*? I'm entitled to choose what we do too, *aren't I*?' But though there is control in this tactic, forcing answers, it is a dubious power for, in requiring reinforcement of an assertion, it betrays uncertainty, casts doubt on the assertion. Tagging can thus be a nervous, insecure ploy like *hedging*, which involves surrounding otherwise confident statements with anxious-sounding murmurs like 'you know', 'sort of', 'kind of'.

On the other hand, tag questions can be genuinely powerful, and women do take advantage of their *facilitating* potential. That is, a tag question may be posed by a mother to coax a reluctant child, or by a party giver to draw out a shy, nervous guest. A tongue-tied party-goer, asked 'You come from Nottingham, don't you?', will surely risk a response of some kind, confident that at least she knows the right answer to this one! And 'It's time to go to bed now, don't you think?' may disarm a wayward child by drawing him or her into the decision-making process.

Tags can also pressure, even have a hint of menace. It depends on their tone. 'You are going to go to bed now, aren't you?', can, depending on the intonation and stress patterns with which the utterance is delivered, be more effective than a command!

But, of course, the roles of party giver and of mother are positions of some sort of power (though feminist thinking might want to argue that a mother's power is ambiguous, since it may be 'permitted', even required, by a father, the role dictated by the needs of patriarchy). Furthermore, it has been suggested that it is not gender, but power – whatever its source – that is at the root of conversational difference.

Is it, then, not because of their gender as such, but because women are very often without power in mixed groups that, in such a context, they manifest the kind of 'weak' conversational features that we have just listed – so much so that they have been termed 'women's language'? Furthermore, if this is the case – if weakness or strength are their trigger factors – are such features really restricted to women? Might not men also manifest them? In fact, should we be talking not about *male and female* language but about *powerful and powerless* language?

O'Barr and Atkins (1980) believe so. For, according to their research, if women are powerful, they may use conversation to their advantage – and put men who are for some reason weak at a disadvantage. They observed this kind of language behaviour in American courtroom discourse. If a woman was an expert witness or, outside the court, she was employed in a position of authority, her language was powerful (in the kinds of ways we listed above as 'male'). If, on the other hand, a male witness was at some disadvantage during the proceedings or, outside the court, was unemployed, or in some other way powerless, his language was similarly weak (in the kinds of ways mentioned above as possibly 'female').

So, which perspective of men, women and language is nearer to actuality in the playing of this Game? If observers note differences in the players' linguistic performances, differences that match or contrast with so-called 'women's language', are these differences related to gender – or to power? If they do seem to be power-related, does this still account for (but complicate) the widely held belief that women have a particular kind of language?

And if power is the thing, do boys playing this Game in positions of relative weakness – as the failed student, say, or the 'fairly new' teacher – think they are using language less strongly than they believe, being boys, they would normally choose? Do the girls feel they usually use weak language but, if cast in a particularly powerful role, find themselves slipping into stronger talk?

Answers to questions such as these cannot be predicted with any certainty, given the number of related variables. For instance, the parent could be played as a father or a mother and there is no guarantee which of these parental roles the students will see as powerful or powerless [see Tutor and Student Comment (a), pp. 85–6]. But this very unpredictability is one of the Game's lessons. It illustrates the complexity of sociolinguistic issues and warns against drawing hasty and simplistic conclusions. Overall, instead of providing answers, this Game, like many others in this series, raises questions for debate.

In addition, it can give students a chance to experience unaccustomed weakness, or power, and allow them to practise a kind of language which may be unusual for them [see Tutor and Student Comment (b), p. 86].

N.B. Another approach to language and gender is the argument that women's language is intrinsically different in ways that, though possibly weak in relation to 'male' discourse, are none the less valuable. These include cooperative, supportive group discourse. The whole subject is extremely complex and readers might like to read much further. Good starting points would be Cameron (1985), Coates and Cameron (1988) and Cameron (1991).

Sequel

Boys, girls and oral exams

It might be interesting to discuss the language that girls and boys think is expected of them in oral examinations (GCSE English, for example). For, if some students choose the kind of language traditionally assumed to belong to women (the language women may even prefer), they may not do well in the exam – for they could then be colluding in their own silencing and silence cannot be marked! Simultaneously, these same students, by using facilitating language that encourages others in their group to talk, may be helping the already powerful to do particularly well. The boys in one local school told a research student at Loughborough University (Emma Dowson 1988) that they believed their teacher was looking for someone who 'talked a lot', whilst the girls thought a good oral candidate was 'a good listener'!

Afterword

Game plan

(a) The imagined context of this Game, particularly the likely consequences of the failed grade, will clearly need adjusting according to the age and experience of the participants. When higher education students are playing, we imagine the Head of Department's office in the Law Department at Barchester University. It is the summer term of finals year. The student has failed a crucial paper: this means he or she cannot proceed to law school next term and must return to re-sit. The consequences for grants and future career prospects are dire.

(b) Single-sex groups can play this Game. They can try to assess whether or not playing an unaccustomed role or changed gender, or a combination of the two, affects their language.

(c) A few props may help. Chairs and tables are likely to be on hand to create the office scene, and giving a student who is playing 'mother' a handbag to clutch does wonders for the acting!

Tutor and student comment

(a) King Edward VII Community College sixth-form students found the power/powerless theme in this Game a good follow-up to **Winning words**

[Sequel to **Cracking the Joke!** (2.5)], which they chose to play first. It was a helpful focus for their thoughts after reading a recent paper on language and sexism.

(b) Though there is no 'stage direction' giving clues to the gender and character of the parent in this Game, it is intriguing how often groups cast the parent as mother – and a very powerful, linguistically forceful mother at that. The Game's head teachers – male and female – frequently quail before her.

(c) This Game teaches as much about linguistic method – particularly the need to define and identify variables precisely and minutely, and also the complex nature of sociolinguistic evidence – as it does about language itself. Our students tend, before we start, to be simplistically adamant that women are automatically and inevitably disadvantaged by male use of the English language. One male student, in particular, in some ways extremely able and politically aware, tended to be irritated by linguistics: 'Why bother dissecting the language – I know what's happening in society without doing that'. But, having been persuaded to play, he was more ready on subsequent occasions to look for linguistic evidence of his assertions.

(d) We had a student who, being very intelligent and self-confident, dominated classes. He was only too ready to hold forth scathingly and at length about the patriarchal oppression of women. But, after playing this Game, it occurred to him that his own language performance might be contributing to the problem! His insight [which increased when he played **Winning words**, the Sequel to **Cracking the Joke** (2.5)] helped to make subsequent discussions in which he took a less one-sided part.

(e) Another male student in this same group [see (b) above] was equally intelligent but less self-confident. He usually said little in seminars and, when he spoke – giving the lie to simple assumptions about gender-related linguistic performance – there was a tentativeness reminiscent of (so-called) 'women's language'. But, when playing the Game, he was cast as the head teacher, and was surprised to hear himself slip easily into what was, for him, an unusually powerful linguistic performance. But his pleasure at feeling an unaccustomed sense of control was mixed with some disquiet that he could so easily, given the authority, become something of a language bully.

2.4 CROSS TALK

Sequel: **SPEAKING**

Focus: Considering *ethnomethodology* and *enthnography*, describing the part we expect language to play in a particular kind of event and recognizing that this varies (sometimes with resultant misunderstandings) between cultures. Work by Hymes (**SPEAKING**) is the subject of the Sequel.

Age range: From 14 years to Higher Education (see Game Plan), younger for the Sequel.

Preparation time: Nothing is essential for **Cross Talk** itself. However, students might tape-record other speech events in order to try out the Sequel to the Game.

Related Games: **Talking Power** (2.3), **Talking 'Proper'?** (2.6), **Shaping Thought** (2.7), **Laying Down the Language Law** (2.9).

The Game

The Game is in two Stages. Stage Two should not be explained to the players until Stage One has been completed.

Stage One
The players should cast from among themselves a middle-aged husband and wife, Mr and Mrs Green. They should also choose students to act as a newspaper reporter called Mr Smith, again middle-aged, and his new and relatively young assistant Ms Jones. The remaining students can divide into two groups, ready to work either as advisers to these role players, or as linguists describing the language behaviour they observe. (If the class is small, those who are not acting can double-up as both advisers and observers.)

Mr Smith, working with Ms Jones, has written a report about the Greens in which, say the Greens, Mr Green is unjustifiably maligned. Letters from the Greens to the newspaper have not produced a retraction of the article. The Greens decide on further language strategies: they arrange to speak their minds in a meeting with Mr Smith and Ms Jones.

The players should act this meeting out. The strategies they might employ should be worked out beforehand, in discussion with those members of the group chosen to act as advisers. (Pre-planning is to some extent out of line with the spontaneity that, as Chapter 2 discussed, is generally important in these Games. However, as the players in **Cross Talk** are not middle-aged, or likely to be very familiar with the offices of newspaper reporters, they will need a little time to think themselves into their roles. But preparation time of this sort is not likely to be necessary in other role plays, like that in **Talking Power** (2.3) for instance, because players are more likely to be personally familiar with the kind of situations they are acting out.)

The rest of the group – those who have been designated observers – should take careful note of the role players' language behaviour. First and foremost they are to look out for assertive, powerful language and particularly to assess the actor(s) who behave(s) most 'pushily'. Assertive behaviour *might*[1] be:

• initiating language exchanges;

[1] See footnote on page 88.

- interrupting others;
- overlapping the ends of other people's remarks;
- taking relatively long conversational turns.

Unassertive behaviour *might*[1] be:

- remaining silent;
- hedging remarks ('It's *sort of* like that');
- using a lot of fillers (like 'you know', 'you see');
- using tag questions ('I should do that, *shouldn't I?*').

Stage Two

Different cultures do not all behave in the same way linguistically. For instance, if silence greets a proposal of marriage in England, the pause probably indicates uncertainty. If the same thing happens in Japan, however, the silence is taken as an acceptance! (see Wardaugh 1986: 234–7 for other examples). It would not be surprising, then, if a meeting to sort out a complaint like the Green's involved, in a different culture, different language behaviour.

In Malagasy, for example, as Elinor Keenan's study shows (Katriel 1986), women are required to initiate any necessary verbal confrontations because linguistic directness and aggression is disvalued – and therefore avoided by men who see themselves as the more subtle and sensitive sex. There seems to be a definite linguistic cultural contrast here, between Malagasy and ourselves.

The players should therefore continue to imagine themselves as the Greens and Mr Smith and Ms Jones, but now, again directed by their advisers, re-play their roles as if they were people of a culture in which women are expected to be linguistically assertive and men normally remain in the language background. Mrs Green will have to take up the dispute, and Ms Jones, despite/because of her sex, will have to respond assertively. Mr Smith and Mr Green cannot be aggressive. This language behaviour should be carefully described by the observers (who will again look for the kinds of features listed above).

The Point of the Game

This Game is not designed to illustrate Malagasy language behaviour as such: the above description of this behaviour is very broad and simplified. The role plays are intended merely to increase awareness, in principle, that culturally

---

[1] These features of powerfully *assertive* and *unassertive* language are described in more detail in the Point of the Game following **Talking Power** (2.3). However, it must be remembered that there is not a strict correlation between the form language takes and its meaning. For instance, remaining silent may well be the mark of unassertiveness, of insecurity perhaps, but it can also be used as a powerful ploy: a person trying to explain something delicate, or controversial, can be unnerved – deliberately – by a co-conversationalist who remains totally and coldly silent while the speaker plunges nervously on. Observers will therefore need to interpret signals sensitively and in relation to other aspects of the language behaviour they are hearing.

related language differences do exist. The Game is thus related (see above) to others which have 'difference' at their core. It will therefore be interesting to see who, in the British scene, instinctively took the verbal leads – Mr or Mrs Green, Mr Smith or Ms Jones. If Mr Green and Mr Smith were the aggressors – and this possibility might be increased by casting them as middle-aged and, therefore, perhaps, less affected by feminism than younger men! – the point about cultural difference will have been made by contrast with the Malagasy situation. If, on the other hand, the women took the western lead, then interesting questions are raised about just what *is* accepted western male/ female language behaviour nowadays. Queries also arise about how definitive our linguistic statements regarding norms can be, and also about cultural change and its linguistic counterparts. Try casting the home-grown Ms Jones first as 16, then as 26, and finally as 56, listening to see if there is there is any difference in her language behaviour.

As for the 'Malagasy' actors, their feelings, as they tried deliberately to act out non-western behaviour, will provide food for thought (see Tutor and Student Comment, below). It must be stressed of course that, despite their role playing, the situation in which they act is cast (unless someone in the group has special knowledge and can direct an authentic setting) in a very western image. However, as already mentioned, the exercise is not intended as an insight into genuine Malagasy behaviour: it is a means of experiencing unfamiliar communicative behaviour and thereby realizing that different ways of 'languaging' are possible, indeed likely. It is a complex matter. As Gumperz (Gumperz and Hymes 1972: 15) writes:

> Communication is not governed by fixed social rules: it is a two-step process in which the speaker first takes in stimuli from the outside environment, evaluating and selecting from among them in the light of his own cultural background, personal history, and what he knows about his interlocutors. He then decides on the norms that apply to the situation at hand. These norms determine the speaker's selection from among the communicative options available for encoding his intent.

This selection procedure is the concern of *ethnomethodology*, a branch of sociology dealing with cultural 'know how', the commonsense knowledge which people need to possess in order to survive in their particular society. Part of the knowledge involved is frequently linguistic (see, e.g. Garfinkel, in Gumperz and Hymes 1972: 301–324).

For instance, we know how to behave at a wedding, but this knowledge differs from culture to culture. If we do not use language in our culture's expected way, we shall not 'fit in'. On the other hand, if we do 'fit' our own people, we may be at odds with others. Trudgill (1983: 131–2) describes conversational conflict in Western Canada between English-speaking people of European origin and speakers of Athabaskan, a group of North American Indian languages. The latter do not speak until they are certain of social relationships: the former speak readily when meeting new people precisely in order to make those relationships. Therefore, because the Indians tend to remain silent, the English speakers (playing their own particular language game) talk on and on, trying to make contact and to fill the silence which they (but not the Indians) find uncomfortable. And, unless the two groups realize that different peoples behave differently through language, they part company each thinking the other rude.

Players of **Cross Talk** may, particularly after its Stage Two, wish to consider the misunderstandings that can arise when different peoples, with traditionally different language behaviour, meet to talk and may be confused by, or unaware of, conflicting norms. Moreover, members of a multicultural class might generate particularly interesting and valuable discussion about differences in their own language use, and its social consequences, within their own culture and others.

Wherever possible, when such differences are within their personal experience, students should go beyond the generalized comment which is sufficient to establish the Game's basic Point about cultural relativity, trying instead to describe the behaviour they are discussing in explicit *ethnographic* terms. An *ethnography* is a description of a language event: it describes in considerable detail the factors that define a piece of language behaviour according to its participants' expected norms. Description of this kind is discussed below in the Game's Sequel.

Sequel
SPEAKING
The two scenes, particularly the Malagasy one, are imaginary and intended to introduce a general principle. However, students might try to describe a real language encounter, of their own experience in their own culture, through an ethnographic framework.

Hymes (Gumperz and Hymes 1972: 35–71) has suggested a convenient acronym, SPEAKING, for the factors he considers essential to include in a linguistic description of such an event. Roughly (for a very helpful summary, see Wardaugh 1986), these are:

- the *Setting* and *Scene* of the event (set in Buckingham Palace, the scene an audience, say, or an investiture);
- its *Participants*;
- the *Ends* or *goals* these participants have in mind as a result of their language, and the outcomes which ensue;
- the *Acts* – form and content – of language used by the participants;
- the *Key* to the exchange, its tone, manner or spirit;
- the *Instrumentalities* involved, like voice or writing, and dialect, register, etc;
- the *Norms* that are expected, e.g. turn-taking or everyone talking at once;
- the *Genres* involved.

[Interestingly, Hymes points out that this code word and its referents are not themselves ethnocentric, for they could be substituted by the French PARLANT – *participants*, *actes*, *raison*, *locale*, *agents*, *normes*, *ton*, *types* (Gumperz and Hymes 1972: 65).]

Producing all these aspects of language, in order to 'fit in' to an event, is clearly a very skilled and complex behaviour. For instance, take our culture's understanding of a school lesson. The *scene* will usually be *set* at an appointed time and in an appointed place that is likely to include conventional classroom furnishings: trying to teach sitting on the grass under a tree on the occasional hot day in England is unusual and, with wasps, poison ivy and distracting passers-by, potentially problematic – but it would not be at all odd in, say, some African communities. Teachers and students will be *participants* in classes, sometimes as speakers, sometimes as listeners. Teachers hope, in the *end*, to increase their pupils' knowledge and understanding: it is assumed – but not guaranteed! – that their students will share and achieve this aim. Teacher and students may *act* out language about expected topics in expected ways, delivering particular 'content' in particular 'forms' (see Burton 1980; Sinclair and Coulthard 1975): a geography lesson could include the teacher asking questions and expecting answers from students about the weather in different countries. Would any other kinds of act be possible? The *key* to the lesson will probably vary according to the personalities and/or subject matter involved: friendliness, sarcasm, pomposity and seriousness, any or all of these might be present (though it would be interesting to consider whether this range, particularly relaxed friendliness, has always been acceptable in the school room). Both speech and writing can be *instrumental* in a lesson, and manners of speaking (e.g. Standard or Non-standard dialect) may vary. It would be *normal* in some classes for students not to make a great deal of noise and not to talk much between themselves, but this could vary according to age and to topic. A lesson might include specific categories or *genres* of language, like a poem, or a scientific journal, and it might itself make use of a genre like that of debate or, in the case of learning mathematical tables, of chanting. (Elsewhere, a lesson can be seen as a genre in its own right. A driving lesson, a swimming lesson, and so on, are identifiable as 'lessons' in speech events quite apart from the classroom setting.)

If students or teachers had expectations of this kind, but what happened in class did not follow roughly this SPEAKING description, something would have gone wrong: it would not be what they considered a 'real' lesson. However, this particular description is based on my personal experience and memories of classrooms. Perhaps it does not precisely match present-day students' experience. If not, in what ways would their description differ from mine?

Using the SPEAKING approach, students could describe an interview situation, or a church service, or perhaps a doctor–patient conversation. They could (with the participants' permission) tape-record these language events and then analyse and comment on them for the class as a whole.

They might, next, ask themselves how abnormal, perhaps unrecognizable, their chosen situation would become if one or other of the SPEAKING factors were altered: Would a church service still be a 'church service' if conducted in, say, a cinema or – bearing in mind a nineteenth-century Dorset vicar whose 'parishioners' generally consisted only of his pets, sitting in the front pew – without a congregation? To put it another way, if we changed a conventional SPEAKING aspect of a familiar piece of language behaviour, how far could it continue to fulfil its intended function? If, say, witnesses in a courtroom started to question barristers, instead of confining themselves to answering questions, what would happen to the legal process?

Halliday's (1973) definition of language functions might be considered here. Halliday's argument that children are aware of more functions of language than the adult – who tends to be conscious only of its representational use to inform, and who may forget that it also sets up interpersonal relationships, orders people's behaviour, is imaginative and heuristic – will be recalled from Chapter 1.

The activities described in this Sequel would be a suitable base from which to develop project work. **SPEAKING** could be used to describe and explain language functions that are similar but carried out in different contexts, e.g. buying food in an elegant restaurant, a cafe and a fast-food drive-in. How far does it matter – practically and psychologically – if you do not know the very different language ropes needed to achieve a similar end in any one of these situations?

Afterword

Tutor and student comment

The girls in our group found it extremely difficult to be aggressive when playing Malagasy women in Stage Two. They did become a bit more assertive than they had been in Stage One, but they remained relatively polite and reasonable. They were surprised by this reaction, especially when they had no difficulty in behaving aggressively on a day we were short of boys and they role-played British Mr Green and Mr Smith. Perhaps it is especially difficult to leave the gender roles of our own culture behind, for the students were clearly able to be aggressive, but could only behave in such a way so long as they were 'male' and acting out a familiar stereotype. It may have been particularly hard to forget this stereotype because, although the students tried to imagine themselves as Malagasy people in one essential language respect, we had insufficient knowledge of the culture to set an authentic scene, and the role play must to a large extent have been bound and influenced by our British room and British audience. Whatever the precise reasons, the students' response would seem to emphasize the strength of culturally related language patterns.

2.5 CRACKING THE JOKE!

Sequel: **Winning words**

Focus: Cooperative and non-cooperative conversation considered in relation to 'face', 'force' and 'maxims'.

Age range: From 14 years (possibly younger) to Higher Education.

Preparation time: For **Cracking the Joke!**, it would be helpful (but not essential) to have on hand comedy scripts like those in *Up To You, Porky: The Victoria Wood Sketch Book* (Wood 1985) or to have available a similar (see Point of the Game) pre-recorded television or radio comedy routine. For the Sequel, **Winning words**, copying the 'winning' scripts given below would be helpful.

Related Games: **Talking Power** (2.3), **Cross Talk** (2.4).

The Game

The Game is in two Stages. The Point should be explained after Stage One and before Stage Two.

Stage One
Students should try to work out why the following exchanges may be funny.

(a) *Diner:*   Waiter, what's this fly doing in my soup?
   Waiter: It looks like the breast stroke, sir.

(b) *Customer:*   Hello, there's a pair of red shoes in the window.
   Assistant: That's right. We do that because it's a shoe shop.
                                                (Wood 1985: 55)

If students think they have the formula for these jokes, they should try to articulate it and then have a go at making up other exchanges on the same lines. They should do this before going on to discuss the Game's Point *prior* to experimenting with its Second Stage.

The Point of the Game

The Game, and its Sequel, help to demonstrate that our communicative competence is, in a loose sense, 'rule-based', i.e. we have habits and conventions which we recognize as usual in certain contexts [see, e.g. **Cross Talk** (2.4)], so usual that we know, as speakers or hearers, when we are choosing to manipulate or ignore them (as in the jokes of Stage One).

For instance, a basic, very general principle of conversation is that it is *cooperative*. We seem to expect it, by definition, to follow the kind of principles that Grice (1975) has called 'maxims'. That is, as conversationalists, we would expect ourselves and others to, ideally, hold to the maxim of *quantity* and generally not give too much or too little information. And we would hold to the maxim of *quality*, i.e. as a rule, we would not say what we think is false or something for which we have insufficient evidence. There is also the maxim of *relation* or relevance: would we not, in ideal exchanges, go off at a tangent from the conversation's established path. Then there is the maxim of *manner*, in that, as a rule, we would try not to be ambiguous and to be as brief and as clear as we could. This is the ideal model (see also Wardaugh 1986: 28–84).

But, in real life, discourse is not ideal and rarely precisely follows patterns and models. And yet we must have some sense of these maxims at the back of our minds when conversing, for if they are not taken account of we feel that something odd is going on – just as the audience did when Victoria Wood, playing the role of customer, said to assistant Julie Walters something like:

Hello, there's a pair of red shoes in the window.

and Julie Walters answered, apparently flouting maxims of quantity and relevance and also, in a sense, manner:

That's right. We do that because it's a shoe shop.

(Wood 1985: 55)

(I am indebted to The Nottingham Trent University Communication Studies students who drew my attention to Victoria Wood's scripts.)

There is, moreover, a sense in which maxims are rules made to be broken, for flouting them is not only sometimes at the root of entertaining comedy, it is also involved in sarcasm, irony and – as we shall see in the Sequel – in the manipulation of others.

But another concept, that of 'face', is also important in the shoe shop sketch. Goffman (1976) has said that when conversing with each other, we are involved in 'face-work', constructing and maintaining for each other images and roles. That is, we present and try to preserve our own face. At the same time, normally, we talk in ways which help to protect our co-conversationalist's face. Imagine that one person in a conversational exchange is presenting the face of 'teacher', the other is presenting the face of 'student'. If the student speaks in ways which ignore the authoritative face that is this particular teacher's norm, he or she may come over as cheeky. If a teacher is speaking to a student's parent, however, on this occasion not one but two authoritative faces are involved. But they are authoritative in subtly different ways. Each person, teacher and parent, needs – for a cooperative exchange – to preserve the other's particular kind of power; that is, each will need to acknowledge the other's special, but *different* relationship with, and knowledge of, the student concerned (see also Wardaugh 1986: 284–5).

Some of the humour in the Wood/Walters exchange seems to depend on 'face-work' – or, rather, the perversion of it. Victoria Woods, behaving quite conventionally, takes on the face of customer. She seems, perfectly sensibly, to have 'read' Julie Walters's face as that of shop assistant, for she apparently assumes that she is saying all she needs as customer (observing the maxims of quantity and manner, that is) when she simply states that there are shoes in the window. If Julie Walters had accepted Wood's face as that of customer, interested in buying a similar pair, she might have answered, 'I'll get a pair for you to try. What size are you?' But it seems that Walters has read Wood's face quite differently! Moreover, she herself is assuming an unconventional face. She is helpful certainly, as one would expect in the circumstances, but her face is not that of facilitating assistant to enquiring customer; on the contrary, she seems to be taking on the face of teacher to pupil. In consequence, Walters totally flouts any sense we may have of conversational relevance, quantity and manner, coming over as patronizing and slightly dotty.

The flouting is based partly on Walters's refusal to hear the 'force' of Wood's remark. According to Searle (1969), we can perform *illocutionary acts* when we speak. That is, we can 'act out' certain intentions, quite apart from the overt message and form of an utterance. In other words, the message and form of what we say may state, or question, or command, and so on. However, the *force* of our remark – of our illocutionary act – may not be directly matched with the kind of words and syntax we choose. [Searle's thesis is similar to that of Austin's (1962) in relation to 'performative' language (see also Wardaugh 1986: 274–81).]

For instance, we might make a statement, but it is intended to have the force of – to act out – a command. 'It's bed time', stated to a child, usually has the force of an instruction to go to bed. 'Don't you think it's time you cleared up your room?' is structured as a question, but its illocutionary force may be that of a command.

The context in which the remark is made, together with its tone, will usually help to make its force quite clear. But when Victoria Wood made the statement about shoes being in the window, Julie Walters did not acknowledge its intended force, a force which – given the sort of commonsense knowledge of life and language which, as **Cross Talk** (2.4) exemplifies, we all need to function in our culture (Wardaugh 1986: 244–9) – would have told most hearers was the first move in a polite instruction to Walters, as assistant, to fetch a similar pair for the customer to try.

Stage Two
In small groups, the students should now write – and if possible perform for the whole class – a comedy routine based on flouting maxims and playing with face and force.

However, flouting or manipulating the maxims we seem to observe at our cooperative best, and adopting unconventional faces, is not always a matter of comedy. The process has functions which are not benign, for we can also play deliberate tricks in order to control a partner in conversation, deviating from the ideal of cooperation in subtle ways.

We have already mentioned the matter of face between parent and teacher when discussing a student. Either person can, if they wish, make life very difficult for the other by refusing to acknowledge, in their co-conversationalist's face, any authority or special relationship with the student concerned. To take another example, doctors, if they choose to assume faces of priest-like authority and mystery, can control and frustrate by refusing to recognize in their patients' faces the authority of common sense or of ownership of their own bodies.

However, all of us, whether or not we are in positions of recognized authority, can and often do choose words that are 'winning' in ways which, as the Sequel demonstrates (but clearly does not advocate), may be distressing and unpleasant.

Sequel

Winning words (three activities)

1 Below are two examples of 'winning' words. In each, one of the speakers assumes a powerful face and regards the other speaker, for one reason or another, as powerless. We can hear this happening as the powerful person apparently ignores maxims and plays with face and force – uses, as it were, winning words. Students should plot the winning tactics – not, of course, in preparation for their own more skilful future use, but so that, able to identify them in their own and other's conversing, they may be in a better position to reject their manipulative effects.

Chinese Chequers

(a script for older students)

Imagine a pair of Higher Education students. The relatively powerless person (PLP) in this pair tries to please the more powerful one (PP). The powerful person has control in the sense that he or she is self-absorbed and apparently not very interested in the other who is clearly attracted to him or her. The PP wrong-foots the PLP throughout, consciously or unconsciously insensitive to his or her face, appearing to manipulate maxims and reacting oddly to the intended force of the other's speech. For instance, he or she chooses not to hear the PLP's introductory statement, about booking a table, with the force of an invitation and thus makes a completely irrelevant response. The PLP, on the other hand, plays the conversation game by the unwritten rules of face and maxim – and, sadly, loses.

PLP: I've booked a table for Chinese on Friday.
PP: Did you hand in my essay?
PLP: Yes I did – but, listen, I booked the Tai Wo for Friday.
PP: Friday! That's the day I'll hear about my grant application.
PLP: So perhaps we'll have something to celebrate at the Tai Wo.
PP: I'll certainly be fed up if I don't get it.
PLP: Yes I know. So will I – for you I mean. But do you like the Tai Wo?

PP: Oh I've had some great times at the Tai Wo. I remember going there once with some people from Oxford Poly. They were doing law, I think – there was this one guy he was just going to Australia and then I think he was coming here to do his postgrad year.

PP: Well, it would be possible. Law here is good. So will you come then?

PLP: Where? Oh – to the Tai Wo!

Child's play

(for younger students but suitable for older ones as well)

Children, we might assume, have limited power beside their parents' greater authority. However, this script includes a child who, unusually (?!), controls through being very thick-skinned, stupid or intentionally rude. He or she (deliberately?) mishears the commanding illocutionary force of his or her parent's statement that it is bedtime: the parent appears to collude in this reduction of his or her own powerful face by hearing the child's 'What time is that?' as a genuine query needing as answer. On television or radio this precocious and powerful irrelevance might be funny: in real life, amusement is the last thing the child would provoke!

Parent: It's bedtime.

Child: Oh! That's interesting. What time is that?

Parent: Eight o'clock. We'll be tired in the morning if we don't go now won't we?

Child: Will you? Well, you two go on then. I'll not be too late myself.

Parent: I mean it's *your* bedtime! Your toys want putting away immediately.

Child: Oh I don't think so. They haven't said so.

2 Now, working in small groups, students might write similarly manipulative scripts, consciously manipulating face-work, force and maxims. If these brief dramas are then performed before the rest of the class, listening students can try to identify their controlling language.

3 As already stressed, this Game is not of course intended to encourage devious methods of control. On the contrary, it is designed to draw attention to these so that we may choose to avoid them ourselves and cope with them more effectively in others. Besides, knowing consciously about face and so on might help us to treat co-conversationalists *more* cooperatively. Therefore, some of the students could try to rewrite 'Chinese Chequers' and 'Child's Play' so that the powerful partner and the precocious child help rather than hinder their co-conversationalists. Other students should then work out in what ways the new cooperative language tactics differ from the old manipulative ones.

Afterword

Tutor and student comment

(a) King Edward VII Community College found this Game worked well and helped their students to understand power and control in interaction.

They played it before **Talking Power** (2.3) and found it a useful lead into this Game.

(b) On the other hand, Tupton Hall School suggested there was, in the Game's earliest version at least, 'a danger of creating semi-abuse'. I have, therefore, in the Game's present form, stressed that its intention is quite the reverse and added some activities to further emphasize this.

(c) Tupton Hall School took the opportunity, while on the subject of matters like illocutionary acts, to play with *phatic communion*, for comments of this sort (like 'Good morning' and 'How are you?') are doing something – acting something out, as it were – as well as saying something. As Malinowski (1923: 15) explained: 'Each utterance is an act serving the direct aim of binding hearer to speaker by a tie of some social sentiment or other.' Tupton Hall School staff drew their students' attention to this kind of language behaviour by encouraging them to, unusually, take greetings literally – for example, giving a complete medical diagnosis, prognosis and intended treatment in answer to 'How are you?'

(d) Students who enjoyed thinking about the Victoria Wood script might like to consider the language of comedy discussed in Nash (1985).

Written or spoken language

2.6 TALKING 'PROPER'?

Sequel: **Mix or match?**

Focus: Standard and Non-standard English in school and the notion of speaking and writing 'properly' (with reference in the Sequel to other languages).

Age range: Junior to Higher Education, including trainee teachers for whom this Game has a particular relevance.

Preparation time: Nil, but this is one Game that must have its Point explained before any of the play begins.

Related Games: **Sounds Familiar** (2.2), **Laying Down the Language Law** (2.9).

The Game

(a) *Imaginary Venue.* A school hall. Students should decide (in the light of their particular interest in the Point of the Game) whether this is a primary, junior or senior school.

(b) *Participants.* Some of the students should role play either parents, past pupils, present pupils, teachers, careers officers, social workers, school governors or local MPs – anyone local who might now, or in the future, be involved with the school children. Other students should act as observers, listening to the discussion that is to take place and being ready to sum up critically its arguments for the class as a whole. (N.B. For once, this Game is primarily about the *content* of the debate, not about the language forms used to convey it.)

(c) *Action.* The participants are meeting to debate the issue of using Standard and Non-standard varieties of English in this imaginary school. Many of its pupils begin their education speaking some Non-standard variety of English. The mix of voices, particularly if the setting is urban with a shifting population and a wide variety of lifestyles, could be considerable.

Imagine that, prior to the debate, a talk has been given to those assembled in the school hall, explaining just what 'Standard' and 'Non-standard' languages are, drawing attention to attitudes that may be held towards these varieties in English, and suggesting possible effects of such attitudes.

Furthermore, in order for this Game to work as it is intended – that is, questioning (as discussed in the Point) attitudes to Standard and Non-standard varieties of language – it will be necessary for the students to have heard the equivalent of this talk. For once, in other words, they will definitely need the Point of the Game explaining before they begin playing. Otherwise, the Game could simply reinforce existing misunderstanding and bias.

Having heard the Point, the questions before the meeting are as follows:

1 Should Non-standard varieties of English be encouraged or discouraged in school? And should the same policy be adopted as regards both written and spoken Non-standard English, or should they be treated differently? For what reasons?

2 If Non-standard varieties are to be encouraged, how should this be done? For instance, should they be used on some occasions (which) by the teacher, even if this teacher normally uses Standard English? [Note that Trudgill (1975: 60) argues that such attempts 'may be interpreted as insincere and insulting by the children'.] Should they be formally taught? If so, should they be taught alongside the Standard? Alternatively, should there be special classes held in the Non-standard varieties, and special classes in Standard English?

3 If Non-standard varieties are to be discouraged, how should this be done?

Trainee teachers playing the Game would probably wish to give particular attention to the *how* of the matter, i.e. how they would implement their chosen policy. They might also consider:

4 The kind of training they feel necessary to prepare them – whether or not they are English specialists – for language work.

The Point of the Game

The role-played debate is likely to highlight and question a variety of different attitudes (including both considered judgements and also unthinking biases) towards the relative value and status of Standard and of Non-standard language: it is an exercise in critical linguistics. It should bring out the difficulties and consequences, both theoretical and practical, involved in arranging teaching programmes that satisfy all concerned.

A language consists, of course, as demonstrated in Section 1, of three basic elements: sound, words and syntax. The term *dialect* refers to a variety of a language in all three respects. The term *accent* refers only to the pronunciation of a variety of a language.

We have generally been taught to *write* the Standard English dialect, i.e. we mostly write Standard words in Standard syntax. But this Standard kind of syntax and vocabulary is difficult to define because it has developed over time and will, like any language variety, continue to develop: what was Standard for Shakespeare is not Standard for us. However, the Secretary of State for Education and Science and the Secretary of State for Wales, in their proposals for the teaching of English to 5–16 year olds (June 1989), suggested it is 'in part defined by the uses to which it is put . . . [that is] for a wide range of public purposes' (para. 4.12). But the operative phrase is 'wide range' because, like any variety of language, the Standard changes [as, for instance, **Variety Performance** (2.1) demonstrates] according to the setting, participants and functions of its situation: even in public it can be formal or informal, descriptive or didactic, serious or humorous, and so on. Moreover, Standard English is not automatically the 'best' kind of language: it can be used rudely, illogically, ambiguously – even in public! Nor is the Standard the original form of English, with all other varieties, or dialects, having been derived from it. Instead, Standard English is itself a dialect, just one more version of the language. In the fourteenth century, there was considerable regional diversity in a written English language that had descended from the Germanic speech of the Angles and the Saxons and had also absorbed Celtic and Latin additions and French influence. But by the sixteenth century, the written form of the language – the *standard* written form, from which ours has developed – was, for reasons discussed below, generally the form then used in London and in the 'Midlands' area (the area which now includes, for example, Bedfordshire, Northamptonshire and Leicestershire).

Now, a very large proportion of us also use Standard English grammar and Standard words when we *speak* as well as when we write. At least, we do so on relatively formal public occasions. But, perhaps at home or in groups of friends of a similar regional or class background, we may prefer Non-standard grammatical forms and Non-standard words that are derived from our region or maybe from our peer group. That is, we can switch between the Standard and a Non-standard variety of English if we wish.

However, even though we write, and may well speak, Standard grammar and lexicon, the great majority of us do not use what might be termed 'Standard' sounds, i.e we do not use the English accent that is normally referred to as 'RP' (RP stands for 'received pronunciation'). Instead, many of us speak Standard grammar and words in the Non-standard accent of our region. And this Non-standard accent, by its contrast with RP, can also signal our class membership, for RP is associated not with any particular region but with an upper class and its associated power and prestige.

In consequence, sound snobbery has existed from at least the time of the first Elizabeth. For example, in his critics' view, Sir Walter Raleigh, 'notwithstanding mastership in style' and entering into conversation with the 'learnedest and politest', apparently let the side down because 'he spake broad Devonshire to his dying day' (Honey 1989: 17).

However, the *Report of the Committee of Inquiry into the Teaching of English* (Kingman 1988) and a first step on the road to National Curriculum requirements for English, urges that no attempt should be made to discourage a pupil's use of his or her own accent: 'speakers may be rightly proud of their regional pronunciation, which identifies where they come from' (ibid.: 14).

Nevertheless, the Report insists (as discussed in Chapter 1) that children at school, whatever the variety of English they have acquired at home, should also learn Standard English *syntax* and *lexicon* as of 'right' (ibid.: 14). For Kingman argues that the Standard dialect (word and syntax) is a powerful facilitator, and it is certainly true that it is a language of vital international communication, of politics and education, a language of vast common currency. (The word 'currency' is significant and will be discussed below.)

But the Kingman Report also recognizes the value of the words and syntax of Non-standard dialects: 'each [variety] has its own authenticity, and to move with facility between them is to develop a versatility in language, a linguistic repertoire, which should be open to all' (ibid.: 7). Kingman's support of the Non-standard (in all its aspects, sound, word and syntax) was later endorsed by the secretaries of state in their proposals of June 1989: 'The aim is to add Standard English to the repertoire, not to replace other dialects or languages' (para. 4.43). For one thing, as these proposals acknowledge, language 'is an intimate part of individual and social identity' (para. 4.33). Therefore, any attempt to ridicule or repress a person's variety of their first language must be a denigration, even a kind of assault upon that person. In consequence, the secretaries of state are surely right to insist that 'Standard English has to be treated very sensitively in schools . . . not introduced at too early a stage . . . its uses . . . *discussed explicitly* with pupils' (paras. 4.32, 4.36, 4.41).

The italics in this last quotation are my own, intended to draw attention to the stress by Kingman, and these subsequent government reports and recommendations, that all knowledge about language should (as discussed in Chapter 1) be made *explicit* so that its users may be in greater control of their language behaviour. That is, in the case of the Standard/Non-standard issue, pupils should be able to consciously judge when to choose one variety of English or another from their 'linguistic repertoire'. The intention, in theory, is not to brainwash pupils into an unthinking acceptance of a Standard but to empower them, through understanding, to use or reject it at will – in theory.

There are, however, significant difficulties when it comes to putting theory into practice. For instance, the National Curriculum Council Consultation Report notes that not all students are anxious to acquire the universal 'power' of the Standard (NCC 1989: 14):

> The views of the working group on Standard English were accepted by the majority of the respondents without significant reservation. Several schools referred to the difficulties of promoting Standard English when there was little social motivation for the children to learn it.

The point made in this second sentence is not take up in the Report, presumably in the belief, expressed later in the secretaries of state's proposals (para. 4.9), that although social motivation may not be immediately apparent to students in their local environment, the valuable function of Standard English 'as a language of wide communication', 'in the education system and in professional life, in public and formal uses, and in writing and particularly in print', is self-evident.

But *should* it be so valuable? Sir John Kingman's (1988: 14) image of the English language as 'a great social bank on which we all draw and to which we all contribute' recalls my earlier reference to language 'currency'. The point is, *do* we all contribute to its currency? Cameron and Bourne (1989) think not. They ask: '. . . why is it that some people are forced to borrow at exorbitant rates of interest while their own currency lies valueless in a sock underneath the mattress!' Who, they ask, puts up the capital and who controls the rate of exchange? The short answer, in part, is those managing the bank. Fairclough (1989: 56) points out that the Midlands dialect from which Standard English developed was:

> . . . associated with the merchant class in London at the end of the medieval period. This underlines the link to capitalism, for these feudal merchants became the first capitalists, and the rise of standard English is linked to the growing power of the merchants.

The invention of printing helped to spread the vocabulary and syntax of this form of English. Caxton's press used the dialect to print texts of power and authority – the Bible, literature, law, political pamphlets – setting the seal on its written prestige while its powerful speakers gave its accent cachet and at the same time denigrated alternatives.

The reasons that this particular form of the language became powerful had, then, nothing to do with its intrinsic qualities. Yet sociolinguistic research (Honey 1989: 60) shows that some Non-standard English users are themselves convinced that their own varieties are of limited worth. They imagine them [as discussed in **Sounds Familiar** (2.2)] markers of pleasant personalities – friendly, honest, generous, humorous – but see the Standard as a sign of intelligence, leadership, social status and wealth. However, in terms of form, potential creativity and expressiveness, the Standard has no advantage over any other variety. Non-standard varieties are, by definition as languages, equally rule-governed [see, e.g. **Knowing the Rules** (1.3) and **Jigsaw Puzzles** (1.5)], equally capable of generating spoken and written words and syntax of intelligence, vigour, humour, clarity, authority – and beauty. The nineteenth-century Dorset dialect poetry of William Barnes makes the point; so does Tennyson's Lincolnshire poetry; so does Tom Leonard's twentieth-century Glaswegian writing. [All of these are suggested for work in a Sequel to **Sounds Familiar** (2.2). References will be found in the Bibliography.]

But these poems are rare examples for, since their 'currencies' have been avoided in school and generally disvalued outside, ridiculed and scorned by the powerful and underestimated by some of their owners, Non-standard varieties have not often been written down. In consequence, any permanent, authoritative voices that Non-standard dialects might possess have been, and may continue to be, eroded.

Honey (1989: 173) 'mourns their passing', believing it inevitable. But need it be? (For a highly critical response to Honey by A.D. Edwards, see Mercer 1988.) The Kingman Report, acknowledging the psychological and communicative value of the Non-standard, could herald some change in attitude. Yet this will happen only if the lip-service paid to Non-standard forms is translated in schools (and elsewhere) into a vigorous regard – theoretical and practical – for such varieties. But will there be time? Will there be the inclination?

The secretaries of state's proposal that 'Non-standard usages should be treated as objects of interest and value' (1989, para. 4.42) suggests they may be appreciated rather as precious antiques, to be admired but not much used. And even though Kingman recognizes the intrinsic value of the Non-standard, his report stresses the need to write in *Standard* English, while the secretaries of state propose (para. 4.38) that by the age of eleven 'there should be the expectation of Standard English in written work when appropriate'. Moreover, the National Curriculum (p. 3) insists (apropos of speaking and listening) that from 'level 7, pupils should be using Standard English, wherever appropriate, to meet the statements of attainment'. The point then is, will there be the opportunity, energy and desire, on already crammed timetables, to introduce and encourage anything else, 'wherever appropriate'?

There should be if National Curriculum guidance is followed (DES and WO 1990: 27). Older pupils

> . . . should be helped to recognise that attitudes to Standard English and to non-standard varieties . . . can be based on stereotypes and prescriptive judgements.

And it is true that there are moves in this direction. The recent appearance of Tennyson's Lincolnshire poetry on GCSE examinations (MEG 1989) is presumably an acknowledgement of its Non-standard worth. But stereotypical attitudes die hard, and parents and teachers – and pupils – will need to be convinced of the value of both the Standard and the Non-standard if the spirit of the Kingman Report is to be translated into reality.

Until now, varieties of English have developed alongside each other relatively informally, through historical accident and through social power. But the National Curriculum is a more formal kind of language planning, resembling the kind of government language planning that has taken place in other countries [see **Laying Down the Language Law** (2.9)]. It remains to be seen how powerful an effect its directives will have. Will they simply reinforce the Standard at the expense of the Non-standard? Will they reinforce the Standard, yet value the Non-standard and give students the power to select from the range as they wish? If this second possibility happens, the Standard would become more a language of communicative efficiency and convenience, less a marker of supposed superiority possessed by a powerful élite.

Sequel

Mix or match?
A similar role play could debate a related issue. If the Game's imaginary school is in a multiracial area, its pupils might, at home, speak neither Standard nor Non-standard English, but perhaps a Creole English or some quite different language – or switch between a combination of these. Should a mix of languages and language varieties be encouraged in such a school, in the belief that languages are closely bound up with identity while yet recognizing that an English channel of cross-cultural communication is essential? Would such a policy mean that students speaking English as their first language should be required to learn something of the other languages spoken in their multiracial school? Or should Standard English be encouraged to the exclusion of all variation?

Of course, the situation described here will not be imaginary for many students. It will relate to the position in their own school and it may be possible to take this opportunity to discuss the policy already adopted there.

Afterword

Tutor and student comment

(a) This Game, as might be expected, worked very well with BEd students who pooled the knowledge they had gained, while on teaching experience, from a variety of different schools having different language populations and policies.
(b) Charles Keene College students entered into the Game with gusto. The written work which followed was good.

2.7 SHAPING THOUGHT

Focus: Persuasive stylistic choice and, also, the Whorfian hypothesis.

Age range: The basic Game can be played from a relatively young age but the delicacy of its stylistic analysis, and understanding of its Point, will of course increase with the maturity of the player. Its Point is made initially with the emphasis on choices of words. But it goes on to look more closely at syntactic choices and does so in the context of the Whorfian hypothesis and its implications for determining thought and meaning *within* a language as well as, relatively, between different languages. Racism and sexism are discussed and some reference is made to stylistic choice in psychotherapy.

Preparation time: Nil.

Related Games: Virtually all the Games are relevant to this one since every aspect of language behaviour involves 'choice' from its possibilites of 'style'. But **Knowing the Rules** (1.3), **Identikits** (1.4), **Jigsaw Puzzles** (1.5), **Language for Living** (1.8), **Talking 'Proper'?** (2.6), **Form and Focus** (2.8) and **Laying Down the Language Law** (2.9), are particularly pertinent.

The Game

(a) Players should divide into two groups. Each group is to imagine that it consists of newspaper employees – journalists and editors. The students should each play a specific role. Each group represents a different newspaper, aimed at a different readership, and its editors should decide on its policies.

(b) Both groups are given the bare bones of the same situation. These essentials should include a sequence of events, the people involved in them, the place in which events occurred, the time at which they happened, and any of their obvious, indisputable consequences: these details should avoid any assessment or judgement of the event [see (e) below]. We had decided to play this Game at 11 o'clock one Thursday morning, and then, a little before we were due to begin, we heard the news that Margaret Thatcher had resigned. We now had perfect material for the basics of our story: the people, the time, the place, the inevitability of a new and radically different line up for the leadership contest.

(c) Each group is to report the given situation, turning its bare bones into a story which will engage readers' attention. Each should construct headlines and a story for their front page, choosing their language while bearing in mind editorial policy and readership.

(d) Now the sets should exchange stories. They should read the story they receive and note their reactions. For instance:

- What is the group's impression of the people involved in the story?
- What do they take to be the impact/consequences of the events described?
- What aspects of the story seem to be given prominence?
- Individual stories will probably suggest further questions of a similar kind.

(N.B. Answers may differ within each group. Although there is likely to be a consensus view on a general level, there is no guarantee that readers, because they bring different personal experiences and attitudes to bear upon the text, will respond in precisely the same way to its language choices.)

(e) Students should now ask themselves: 'What aspects of language gave rise to our responses?' For example:

- What sort of individual words, including nouns, adjectives, verbs and adverbs, have been selected? How had these readers reacted to them?
- Are there any particularly significant sounds or rhythms in this piece?
- What similes and metaphors have been used? What was their impact?
- What kind of syntax has been chosen? What part did it play in reader response? (This will be the most difficult question to answer and is intended for the more advanced students.)

If there was a divergence of opinion when answering the questions under (d), this discussion could be particularly stimulating.

(f) Finally, the two groups should compare the language choices of the two pieces and their reader response. They should consider how far the different choices of language, influenced by the different needs of the two papers, may have resulted in significantly *different* ideas and images about the events described. That is, how far has contrasting 'style', in the sense discussed in the Point of the Game, offered contrasting meaning?

The Point of the Game

(a) Stylistic choice

Comparison between the players' stories should demonstrate how very different may be the perception of events, formed by readers, according to the language in which these events have been described – according, that is, to the way in which the language has been *styled*. I am using 'style' to mean any aspect of language choice. And I am suggesting that style is not just the icing on the cake, not just an alternative way – more or less formal, more or less elegant, more or less dispassionate, and so on – of saying the same thing. On the contrary, style *is* the cake: stylistic choice is meaningful choice and thus, more often than not, a change of word, syntax or sound can crucially alter meaning. Changes of style may be changes of *sense*.

Moreover, although the Game works with newspapers, its Point is applicable to any kind of language, and to any kind of language user. Because it is not only journalists, but all of us who can and do make significant stylistic choices as **Knowing the Rules** (1.3) illustrates, the potential for creative choice is a defining aspect of all human language and its users.

But to return to newspapers. During the Gulf War, for instance, *The Guardian* (23 January 1991) gave two lists of language choices, particularly individual word choices, apparently implying that some patriotic British journalists attributed one set of choices to the allies and used the other to describe the Iraqis. According to these lists, nouns chosen by British journalists to label our forces would include *boys*: the enemy, on the other hand, would be referred to by these same journalists as *troops* or *hordes*. Adjectives describing our boys would include *confident, loyal, brave*: their troops would be called *fanatical* or *ruthless*. As for verbs, our brave boys would '*fly* into the jaws of hell': their fanatical hordes would '*cower* in concrete bunkers'. Ours would *neutralize* but theirs would *kill*. The two contrasting lists thus emphasized the powerfully different images that language can create.

However, the title quotation which covered both lists, 'Mad dogs and Englishmen', underlines – since *both* mad dogs and Englishmen went, according to Noël Coward, out in the midday sun – a sameness in the reality behind these two linguistic, stylistic façades. But the incompleteness of the quotation, as used in the headline, seems to me to symbolize the incompleteness, the partialness (in both senses of the word) of the perceptions lying behind the contrasting lists. In this way, the headline draws attention to a tragic irony of sameness. Forces from both sides are sent out to meet the heat of a battle which, in the final analysis, has little to do with perceptions encouraged by language and does not discriminate. Theirs, the title implies, is a shared madness: the adjective 'mad' should apply to both sides – if not to the forces in the field, to those who send them there.

The bare bones of the story described by these words are, then, much the same, however you look at them: human beings and a battlefield. But 'style' your language to talk or write about these bare bones differently (choose differently from the options of its systems of sounds, words and syntax) and you may flesh them out with totally different images and ideas, just as the students will have done in their newspaper reports.

Older students could now go on to think about Point (b) and some related activities.

(b) The Whorf–Sapir Hypothesis: Linguistic determinism and
cultural relativity
The relationship between language and the way we understand our world was the focus of work by the American linguist Edward Sapir (1884–1936) and his student Benjamin Lee Whorf (1897–1941). The Whorf–Sapir hypothesis of linguistic and cultural relativity (based particularly on investigation of American Indian languages) suggests that we perceive the world according to

the language we use to think, talk and write about it: different cultures have different languages and, therefore – so the *strongest* version of the hypothesis would go – they also have *relatively* different understandings of the world as *determined* by their particular language.

Just before the Gulf War, Sari Nasir, Professor of Sociology at the University of Jordan, remarked on Saddam Hussein's choice of the word *daif*, translated as 'guest', to refer to the hostages (the allies' alternative choice of word) held by Saddam against their will. The hypocrisy – as the West perceived it – of the word 'guest', caused offence and distress. Sari Nasir, however, argued that:

> For you, a guest is someone you ask into your home. For us, the word *daif* means someone who is already in your home. Even today, if a man kills your child, by accident or by design, he may claim sanctuary in your house . . . and you must give him hospitality, food, protection, until the mediation begins.
>
> (quoted in *The Guardian*, 3 November 1990: 27)

Now it is true that neither culture, without this kind of explanation, is able to comprehend the other's choice of word and the alternative point of view it expresses. Moreover, it is only a short step from the linguistic relativity of different cultures to that of comparative texts in the same language – to English language newspapers, in the case if this Game. If you read only the language of your usual morning paper, you will become accustomed to its usual language and the usual world view 'styled' by the linguistic choices of its particular 'discourse': you will remain unaware of the alternative language and alternative perceptions available in other papers.

But of course, no newspaper, no one's choice of language, need have the last word: experience, or deliberate alternative speculation or alternative reading, can contradict the images created by the language of a particular newspaper or any other genre – just as knowledge of both Arab and western cultures and their relative languages could elucidate the *daif*/guest/hostage issue. So the crucial point in this case is whether or not Saddam Hussein himself knew the distressing implications of his word when translated into English, whether those making it knew both the precise nuances of *daif* and those of the English 'guest'. For words are useless, inert, without their human users. Those who write, speak – and read or listen – invest them with meaning, grant them or deny them power.

Besides, human linguistic creativity [which is a subject of other Games, including **Jigsaw Puzzles** (1.5) and **Language for Living** (1.8)] prevents any language from being a permanent strait-jacket upon thought: no language is finite for it is constantly developing in response to changing understanding in a changing world, and sometimes hastening the change. So the *weaker*, and most people would agree more acceptable, version of the Whorfian hypothesis, is that a language does not restrict its users to a certain world view, permitting no other – but *encourages* that view.

For example, in the course of Gulf War coverage, civilians learnt, perhaps for the first time, of 'smart bombs'. The noun phrase was used[1] in the wake of reality, labelling a weapon *after* it had come into existence, but it also played a part in *creating* the new reality of a new attitude to war. For the phrase fosters a belief that now, in war, the need for human life to inflict death or to suffer it is minimized by a precise technology that has – literally, the stylistic choice implies – a mind to win: it is 'smart'. Of course, reading the phrase does not oblige us to take its point. But, once read, we shall need – if we wish – to make a conscious effort to reject its implications of easy victory.

(c) Style and prejudice
Without a conscious effort to reject their effects, language choices can also inspire and maintain (i.e. determine) sexism and racism.

Using the pronoun 'he' or the word 'man', when *both* men and women are intended, can – unless the hearer of these words makes a deliberate effort to understand a dual gender reference – contribute to female invisibility. And there are words referring to women which have traditionally carried negative connotations, whereas the male equivalent did no such thing, e.g. master/ mistress, landlord/landlady. Such words will continue to carry their old implications (what, precisely, are these?) unless users and hearers agree to invest them with a changed significance to match a changed perception. The invention of new words, however, can encourage a fresh understanding. Thus the creation of 'Ms' (implying what?) caused a great deal of ridicule and irritation, but irritation means notice taken and notice taken may eventually lead to new attitudes.

The same is true of language choice and racism. We look, in the Sequel to **Jigsaw Puzzles** (1.5), at Rastafarian efforts to reformulate English in a way which seeks to reject racism and to elevate Rastafarian culture.

But there are red herrings in stylistic study if too simplistic an equation is made between words, meaning and power, especially if bits of a text are extrapolated and their significance judged without reference to the whole package. A student pointed out to me that the jealous, murderous Queen in the fairytale of Snow White is traditionally described as 'dark' skinned, at least by comparison with the 'snowy' complexion of her innocent young rival. The student felt there was something racist in modern-day acceptance of this apparently symbolic contrast, particularly in the Walt Disney version of the story. She may be right. But her commendable sensitivity to linguistic racism led her to object every time the tale used the adjective 'black', even when it appeared in a description of Snow White, whose hair was 'black as ebony'. In

[1] A student told me that the phrase came into existence for players of video war games in the 1970s. The point of the video smart bombs was also easy annihilation, a painless clearing of the screen. So for those who knew of this origin, there may have been an even stronger implication in its Gulf usage of war simplified – a game played with sophisticated toys.

this case, 'black' is a stylistic choice tokening great beauty, but the student's wish to prove her point led her to concentrate on individual language choices, in isolation, and to ignore their effect in combination (see also the Afterword).

(d) Styling syntax

So far we have been thinking mostly about word choices. However, the packaging of these into syntactic structure also involves powerful stylistic choice. (A very similar example to the one below is discussed in Chapter 1, but this alternative is included here for convenience: there are obviously as many stylistic possibilities as there are syntactic choices, but what follows is a particularly pointed example which appeals to students.)

Take, for example, the following pair of sentences. [Students should assume that sentence (x) and sentence (y) both refer to the same incident.] Their style, in particular their present-tense verbs and the way they miss out determiners (probably definite or indefinite articles like 'the' or 'a'), immediately signals to readers that they are likely to be newspaper headlines:

(x) Local *cordon bleu* chef poisons couple.

(y) Elderly couple poisoned.

But the syntax hints at much more then genre. For students will probably feel, intuitively, that the two sentences come from different kinds of newspapers, that (x) is from a local paper with an habitual gossipy or scandal-talking flavour, and that (y) could well come from a national paper, maybe a quality national.

In order to explain and to formalize their intuitions students can be asked what they see in response to the first sentence and then what images are trigged for them by the second one. Clearly, no chef will appear in the mind's eye in response to (y): he or she is not mentioned at all. But he or she will be prominent in any mental picture inspired by (x). The couple, on the other hand, will not be clear from (x). Readers of (x) are told nothing about them: we certainly do not know whether they are young or elderly.

The syntactic structures of our two sentences contribute to these contrasting impressions. They 'mean' – and mean persuasively – because the selection of one syntactic form or another draws a reader to one perception or another. How does the grammar do this?

Most importantly, it is working through the grammatical subjects of the sentences. That is, in (x) the chef is the grammatical subject of the sentence, i.e. the participant attached to the verb. But in (y) the couple are the grammatical subject: they are attached to the verb, they are poisoned. Yet the roles of these two grammatical subjects are different. In (a) the chef is, as it were, an actor: he or she does the poisoning. When the grammatical subject is actor, or agent of some kind, then the sentence is technically an *active* one. In (y), however, although the couple are grammatical subjects, they are not actors. On the contrary, they, being poisoned, are acted upon. We could say they have the, syntactic role of 'victims' or 'patients'. This sentence is syntactically, therefore, a *passive* one: the grammatical subject is not the actor but is acted upon.

So it seems that the paper using headline (x) is most interested in the poisoner, the *local* poisoner, and in the act of poisoning. This is probably why we suspect (x) is from a sensationalist newspaper, since it seems part of human nature to be fascinated by the misdemeanours of others we know! The other headline, however, appears less dramatic and therefore this might mean that it is from a 'quality' paper. It seems more distanced from the event, from the perpetrator certainly, for it is evidently less interested than (x) in looking for someone to blame. The 'agent' of the poisoning, the chef, is not even mentioned in this passive syntax.

But he or she could have been. Passive sentence structures allow us to choose whether or not, at the end of the utterance, we make reference to an actor. So it is possible to add on to the end of (y), 'by local *cordon bleu* chef'. Having this choice allows English speakers to turn the spotlight towards, or away from, a 'doer'. But it never, in passive sentences, falls squarely on this actor for he or she will always come last in the sentence while the victim, patient or whatever, literally takes first place. In this case, it is a poisoned couple who first come to mind. And the adjective, *elderly*, makes certain that we envisage a particular kind of couple. In the active sentence, on the other hand, they are inevitably pushed to the back of the stage, edged out by the main character, the poisoner.

As suggested in relation to other Games, Crystal (1988) is very helpful with regard to syntactic metalanguage and this can be used in stylistic description.

However, older students might be introduced to the concept of Halliday's Systemic Grammar (described in *Explorations in the Functions of Language*, 1973). Morley (1985) explains this kind of systemic grammar in detail. But, essentially, Halliday's model of language assumes that every sentence can have three purposes (functions), uttered together like a chord. We signal these through choices made from the available systems of language – sound, word, syntax, intonation and rhythm. There is the *ideational* function, the carrying of information. Different language choices may, as we have been seeing in this Game, present the same piece of information differently. There is the *interpersonal* function which relates speaker to hearer; for instance, asking questions sets up a relationship rather different from that involved in making statements. There is the *textual* function which connects sentences to each other. Textual links are created in a number of ways. For example, if we say or write

The examination results were excellent. This was a considerable relief to him.

it is clear that 'This' makes a bridge between the two sentences, referring back to the excellence of the exam results and that 'him' refers back to someone already mentioned.

(e) Therapeutic choice
The choice of syntax to highlight or turn attention away either from the agent
or from the patient can also play a significant part in the changing perception
which is at the core of successful psychotherapy. Older students might like to
consider a discussion of this in *Language Variety and the Art of the Everyday*
(Shepherd 1990).

(f) Style and metaphor
Language for Living (1.8) is an appropriate Game to play in conjunction
with **Shaping Thought**. The Game is based on a relationship between choices
of metaphor and the shaping of perception. It looks at the way in which, for
instance, we see time as money, argument as battle, love as madness. It also
directs older students to a critique of Susan Sontag's book *AIDS and Its
Metaphors* (1989) and the Afterword refers to the way in which Tupton Hall
School linked the Game with the Whorf–Sapir hypothesis.

(g) Further suggestions
There is clearly not space here to discuss all the possibilities of meaningful
stylistic choices. However, Haynes (1989) would be a helpful text for students from about GCSE level. Blake (1990) would be appropriate for sixth-
forms. Birch (1989) cautions against stylisticians forgetting that their own
attitudes and biases may affect the way they respond to stylistic choices (see
also the Afterword). Carter (1982) and Carter and Simpson (1988) include
examples of stylistic criticism that will be of interest to the more advanced
student.

Afterword

Tutor and student comment
A point touched on above, in connection with stylistic criticism of Snow
White, is worth developing here. However careful and honest one's approach
to stylistic criticism, it must inevitably be informed by one's own cultural and
personal ways of thinking. That this is so, and that there may therefore be a
number of possible responses to a text, will need acknowledging in the carrying
out and writing-up of any critique, but it need not prevent (indeed, it should
facilitate) a consistent and thorough analysis. However, students tend to be
very ready to assume they know what a text means and, whether or not they
have thought through and confirmed this, to impose their own reading on the
piece. Moreover, if not properly carried through, stylistics can reinforce these
incomplete responses and biases. For readers may be quick to spot odd words
and phrases which they are eager to assume confirm their beliefs about a text
(its overt and its hidden meanings) and it can be difficult to persuade them to
look further and to have these beliefs challenged by a more thorough description
and evaluation of the text's stylistic choices as a whole. However, the very fact

that all of this is so, is the strongest argument in favour of stylistic criticism, properly done.

2.8 FORM AND FOCUS

Sequel: **Conversions** (an alternative Game suggested by Tupton Hall School)

Focus: Stylistic 'choice' and its contextual constraints.

Age range: The Game may be adapted for any age.

Preparation time: Nil.

Related Games: **Identikits** (1.4), **Variety Performance** (2.1), **Shaping Thought** (2.7).

The Game

This Game is likely to be most useful if it is played after some preliminary discussion of stylistic 'choice' and its implications. **Shaping Thought** (2.7), which is concerned with the shaping of meaning through language choice, would therefore be a good Game to try beforehand. **Form and Focus** is related to **Variety Performance** (2.1) in that both are about the contextual pressures which influence, and limit, choice of style.

After preliminary stylistic work of this sort, the students should all imagine a new product that has come on to the market – a word processor, washing machine, hair restorer, cat flap or whatever. Then the group should divide into three sub-groups as follows.

- The students in one sub-group are to imagine they are advertising agents: they should write advertising copy for the product.
- The students in another sub-group are to act as instruction manual writers: they should write instructions, directed to buyers, for using the product.
- The third sub-group should imagine they work for *Which?* or a similar journal: they should write a report on the product, assessing its merits.

When these texts are complete, they should be passed around the other groups so that their choices of sound, word and syntax can be compared and contrasted. The reasons for any marked contrasts should be discussed.

The Point of the Game

Each group, because it is working with different purposes and different audiences in mind, will no doubt produce very different kinds of writing. Describing these differences in terms of sound, word and syntax draws attention to our human potential for linguistic choice, but also indicates that this 'choice' is limited, guided by the purpose of the text. [Some ways of describing and analysing style, and titles for further reading on stylistics, are suggested in **Shaping Thought** (2.7).]

For example, the advert has to be persuasive in some way. There are, of course, many linguistic routes to persuasion, but readers might be tempted by language choices which appeal to their emotions, or else to their intellect, or to their pragmatism. In any event, an advert will almost certainly contrast in some stylistic way with the analytical, evaluative language needed for reports that, like those in *Which?*, have to weigh and balance arguments and evidence. As for instruction manuals, these, above all else, will need stylistic choices which aim at foolproof clarity. For instruction manuals are designed to *instruct*, and they should (though they do not always succeed) do so without ambiguity. They cannot risk the wrong button being pushed at the wrong moment! Therefore, this kind of writing needs to be ultra-explicit. A piece of engineering writing might read as follows:

> The head of the small piston has a stellite faced chamber which seats on to a seat on the valve cap forming a front seat for the small piston. An indicator rod is screwed onto the bottom of the small piston.

Students usually find this extract very difficult to read. Perhaps this is because it consists of so many noun phrases: we are invited to visualize a potentially confusing multitude of images. Moreover, the head words of the phrases are technical, so these instructions would only help the specialist. Then again, the noun phrases tend to be repeated, and some (specialists as well as non-specialists) may find this repetition not only visual overkill but also irritatingly unsubtle.

We could, of course, substitute a pronoun the second time a phrase is needed: 'The head of the small piston . . . forming a front seat for *it*'. And we could add interest through choosing alternative words: '*fits* on to a seat'. Because we are accustomed to building our texts up in this kind of way – making them *cohere* by using words and structures which, referring backwards (*anaphorically*) and forwards (*cataphorically*), create links across the sentences – these substitutions would probably make the passage easier to read. But it could be a deceptive kind of ease. For there is always the possibility that these changes, though attractive and easy on the eye and ear, may confuse: we may not make the proper connections. Misunderstand the references being made, through pronouns or alternative structures – select, push, pull, press the wrong 'it, this, that' or 'the other', say – and the engine could fail. [Students will find cohesion and other aspects of style very helpfully discussed in Blake (1990).]

The physical form of the text – to some extent dictated by function, like the language choices themselves – also influences style. For instance, even the size of a business card, menu or newspaper is influential, simply because it limits the number of words possible. Indeed, choices for these kinds of texts tend to become conventions: there are accepted ways of choosing and packaging the words and syntactic structures of newspaper headings and articles, menus or business stationery. A need to lay out language in an attractive, or clear, or eye-catching way on a page (or carrier bag, video pack, pub sign) could also affect the linguistic structures chosen.

Advanced students will wish to develop a much more sophisticated understanding of the relationships between text and context than can be accomplished here. Obviously the pressures which surround the text are not only straightforward dictates of production and audience requirements. The ideologies, both conscious and unconscious, of their creators, also mark the text more – or less – openly in its composition of sounds, words and syntax. Students would find Fowler *et al.* (1979), Kress and Hodge (1979) and Hodge and Kress (1988) helpful.

Conversions (Alternative Game)
Tupton Hall School draw attention to the pressures of function, context and convention upon language choice by asking their students to *convert* texts. That is, students might be asked to change a recipe into a short story, or a legal document, or a piece of health food propaganda. They will need to describe and account for the changes they have made and consider their consequences. Think of the guilt or self-righteousness or starvation that might become associated with a nut roast recipe turned health food polemic!

Afterword

Tutor and student comment
Charles Keene College found this Game helpful. The practice was useful because whilst students had no difficulty recognizing the purposes of texts and could therefore write roughly suitable ones, they experienced difficulty at first in identifying and describing distinguishing features. Conscious deliberation of this kind must increase control of production, and reception.

2.9 LAYING DOWN THE LANGUAGE LAW

Sequel: **Language planning in the British Isles**

(I am indebted to Dr Margaret Sheil, who teaches linguistics at the State University of New York, Oneonta, for suggesting this Game and providing its materials.)

Focus: Language planning.

Age range: From 14 years to Higher Education.

Preparation time: Time to make team copies of relevant information about African countries.

Related Games: **Variety Performance (2.1), Sounds Familiar (2.2) Talking 'Proper'? (2.6).**

The Game

Students should divide into teams, ideally of five or six. The participants in each team should imagine themselves to be African. They are acting as members of a Government Committee which belongs to one of the following developing nations: Tanzania, Burundi, Nigeria, Kenya or Zaïre. If there are five teams, one for each country, so much the better, but the Game will still work if only two or three countries can be considered. One student on each team should act as secretary, noting down committee opinion and decisions in order to pass these on to the whole class after the role play.

Each committee has met to debate and make recommendations about their country's language planning. Either French or English – one or the other having been the language of the colonizer – is the world language in use in each nation playing the Game. But children do not speak their country's world language at home. In the light of this discrepancy, the committee members – who might represent the ministries of education, internal affairs, trade and so on – are to discuss issues surrounding language teaching in school. What language(s) will be taught? What factors must be considered in making a choice? The following is the kind of information that would affect decision making. It would be helpful for each team member to have a copy of these details.

Tanzania: a British protectorate from the end of the first World War until independence. English is the international language used. But Swahili, originally a language of the coastal areas, has been successfully brought into the interior of the country and is now either a first or fluent second language for virtually everyone. It is the official language and is used by the government. Tanzania is also adjacent to countries in which Swahili is used, particularly in urban areas and in multi-tribal areas, as a lingua franca. However, English is at present the language of secondary education. What do government representatives think of this situation?

Burundi: a land-locked, poor country whose world language is French. Until recently, education was, after the primary years, entirely in French (the language of the Belgian protectorate) but all secondary school pupils must study English. However, the native language of Burundi is Kirundi, and refugees from Rwanda speak Kinyrwanda which is mutually intelligible with Kirundi. To the east of Burundi, giving access to the ocean, are Kenya and Tanzania, both using English for international dealings. What do government representatives think should be the relative positions of Kirundi, French and English in education?

Nigeria: Ibu, Hausa and Yoruba are its three major tribal areas. Each have very different cultures and traditions, and each has a different language. Modern Nigeria is a construct made by the British colonizer, and English has been the language of education, particularly at the secondary and tertiary levels. Cambridge examinations in English are taken at two levels. How do government representatives think the indigenous languages should be treated in their respective areas? How should they be regarded in Lagos, the huge and sprawling capital city to which people have come from many areas? How should English be treated?

Kenya: a former British colony which has people of many different tribes. English is the international language, and Swahili – a Bantu language, associated with a region rather than a particular tribe – has spread as a lingua franca. Swahili is taught in the schools from the beginning, and many textbooks have been produced in this language. But English is also still taught and used in education. Do government representatives think this is desirable?

Zaïre: a huge country whose official national language is French. French is taught, as is a little English. In addition, four native languages are official according to province. There is no native language which can be accepted by everyone, because of tribal difference. A dialect of Swahili is used in the eastern province which is near countries where Swahili is used in urban areas (Burundi, Rwanda, Uganda). What do government representatives feel educationalists should be doing?

The Point of the Game

Governments have often felt it necessary, for a variety of reasons, to plan and standardize their countries' languages. The Game invites students to evaluate this kind of planning in the light of their knowledge of language and their understanding of its psychological and pragmatic importance to individuals and to groups [see, for instance, the Point of the Game following **Sounds Familiar** (2.2) and **Talking 'Proper'?** (2.6)].

Take, for example, Norway. Norwegians speak varieties of Non-standard rural or urban dialects. But there are also two, equally official, Standard languages in Norway, used particularly in writing: Nynorsk ('new Norwegian') and Bokmål ('book language'). Bokmål is the language of the majority of books and of the national press. Nynorsk, on the other hand, is the language of the local press and of some literature, particularly that with a rural background. But children learn both, both are used in radio and television, and all official documents are in both languages. The two are mutually comprehensible.

Bokmål has descended from a form of Norwegian heavily influenced by Danish. (Norway was ruled by Denmark from the fifteenth to the early nineteenth century and Norwegian and Danish resembled each other fairly closely.) It is used particularly by the urban upper classes. Nynorsk, on the other hand, which came into being (as Landsmål, 'language of the country') in the nineteenth century, is based on rural dialects, largely uninfluenced by Danish.

In 1938, the government – wanting to bring the two languages closer together – ordered changes in Bokmål school texts that would bring them nearer to the folk-related Nynorsk. There was upper- and middle-class resistance to this move, away from a Standard belonging to the élite and powerful, but in 1959 a new Language Commission took much the same position.

Still, it is hardly surprising that there was opposition to the elevation of Nynorsk. For language is closely linked to cultural identity and to power [cf. the situation in England discussed in **Talking 'Proper'?** (2.6)] . To support the language of a particular group may be to elevate that group's culture at the expense (real or imagined) of another and thus to risk conflict.

To insist on the substitution of any language for someone's first language (not, as we have seen, the course taken in Norway where, though the aim is to bring two varieties closer together, Nynorsk and Bokmål co-exist) can be psychologically damaging and alienating. Frequently, language planning, whether formal or informal, leads to feelings of repression and alienation. In his poem 'The Grafted Tongue', John Montague (1974: 344) wrote of Irish, supplanted in the nineteenth century by English: to have to 'grow a second tongue' can be 'as harsh a humiliation as twice to be born'.

On the other hand, language planning may be pragmatic, even essential. A developing nation will want access to the languages of world knowledge. And its representatives will need to be able to communicate on the world stage.

But there are also practical considerations; for instance the cost and availability of books in local, national and world languages. Students will need to bear all these factors in mind as they role play African government officials.

As for Norway, its two-language situation is expensive and time-consuming, since books must be printed in both, and schools teach both. But, on the face of it, the country's language planning seems to avoid the pitfalls of group rivalry or loss of identity. For, since Bokmål and Nynorsk are both official, Norwegians are free to choose a language in which to write that is close to their own spoken (urban or rural) dialect. However, there was, as already mentioned, opposition to the adaptation of Bokmål towards Nynorsk. Moreover, the very existence of free choice leads, paradoxically, to controversy. For there are significant options to be selected *within* both Bokmål and Nynorsk. That is, each has 'radical' and 'conservative' alternatives for certain words, pronunciations and grammatical constructions. A Norwegian can thus align himself or herself with family and region through selecting and sharing with them Bokmål or Nynorsk. But, at the same time, he or she may make a further linguistic 'statement', a further linguistic alignment, signalling his or her choice of politics through a selection of forms from within either language. Trudgill (1983: 161–6) discusses this intriguing and potentially inflammatory situation in detail. Suffice it to say here that in 1955 a radio weather forecaster lost his job because he chose a radical form for 'snow' instead of a conservative one!

Trudgill (1983: chs 6 and 7) also considers in detail other instances of language planning and of code switching.

Sequel

Language planning in the British Isles

(a) Students might be asked to consider language planning nearer to home by researching the present language situation in Ireland, Scotland and Wales.

   After the 1745 rebellion, the British government prohibited the speaking of Scots Gaelic, the language of the Highlands and the Hebrides. It was allowed into schools after 1918 and in the late 1950s began to be used more extensively as a medium of instruction. However, most secondary school children use Standard English or a local dialect of English.

   Welsh is used more extensively. There has been a bilingual teaching policy for some time and this is re-emphasized in *English and the National Curriculum* (*No.2*) which advises that the 'development of English and Welsh should be seen as mutually supportive' (DES and WO 1990: 43).

(b) Students might also think about the extent to which the Kingman recommendations and subsequent National Curriculum directives about Standard and Non-standard English are instances of 'language planning'. This issue is at the heart of another game, **Talking 'Proper'?** (2.6).

(c) Students playing the Game may well not speak English as a first language. It would be helpful if they could explain to their group how they switch between two or more languages (sometimes selecting one or another, sometimes using first one and then another) and how they feel about the choices they need to make.

Afterword

Tutor and student comment

(a) One student objected that, by playing the Game, participants were continuing a kind of imperialism, making decisions for another country. We stressed that, in order to avoid this kind of bias, the teams were supposed to imagine themselves African and to try to take into account the African point of view. But the student felt that merely contemplating the spread of English was itself a kind of colonialism. We appreciated her point of view but argued that the teaching of English or French is pragmatic, indeed essential if world opportunities are to become available and if vital communications are to be initiated and maintained. We mentioned that a number of African writers choose English in order to open up their perspective on Africa to as wide an audience as possible. And we drew attention to writers like Chinua Achebe who use Standard English alongside a variety of African codes.

(b) Tupton Hall found this Game stimulating, leading into a discussion of English dialect issues. They debated the 'appropriateness' [see **Variety Performance** (2.1)] of using a Non-standard dialect in semi-official spoken contexts like the opening of Parliament, sports commentaries, weather forecasts and chat shows.

4 Projects: The description, analysis and critical explanation of 'real' texts

The Project is now a significant element in a number of General Certificate of Secondary Education and Advanced Level examinations. For instance, the AEB has an English AS Level (985) which requires coursework to include a 2000-word study of an aspect of language 'in use' and the Oxford and Cambridge Board's AS English Language invites a long essay based on the analysis and discussion of 'first-hand experience'. The University of London Board's English Language Studies A Level (174) includes a 3000-word 'practical study' of spoken language in a specific context: the JMB requires something similar. The AEB's Communication Studies A Level (608) also includes project work. As for GCSE, the MEG English Syllabus M offers the possibility of coursework investigating language in use.

However, quite apart from providing a piece of work to assess knowledge, linguistic projects are a helpful approach to language study at any stage, since they involve students in the description, analysis and explanation of real language texts in real contexts: theory meets practice. They are a further rung in the kind of experiential learning, fundamental to *Playing the Language Game*, that can help students to understand – and to assess critically – language behaviour. Because this behaviour is so central to human life, language project work has potential for interdisciplinary study, making links with work in, say, history, sociology, politics and psychology.

Besides, in addition to its specifically linguistic benefits, doing projects can practise a range of skills which unite the 'academic' and the 'vocational'. (This is, of course, true of projects in many other fields as well as the linguistic.) Many of these skills are at a personal level, developing independence and communicative capability. Students may have the responsibility of choosing their own topics. Initiative and determination are needed to overcome unpredictable difficulties. Limited time has to be organized effectively. Places and people have to be contacted for fieldwork. Communication with subjects will need to be tactful and skilful. One student remarked: 'I experienced rather than learned'.

Project work is therefore always original, student-centred work, but language projects will need considerable staff support and advice. The course proper may stop before project work begins, but teaching will continue as original work draws students into fresh areas and fresh methodological and explanatory challenges.

Playing language games can – over and above familiarizing students with the structures of language and linguistic theory – be a helpful preparation for these challenges. Games suggest ideas for investigation and practice of linguistic *description*, *analysis* and *explanation*, three basic steps of project work.[1] Moreover, through encouraging players to ask questions and to re-assess their attitudes to language and its users, games can minimize the danger of a project merely reinforcing limited or biased perceptions.

Still, whatever its benefits, project work is not without difficulty. However, many of the problems that can beset students – and staff – when doing projects, are forestalled by Harris and Morgan (1979). They begin at the beginning, stressing the care that is needed both in selecting suitable texts for analysis and in planning achievable and interesting approaches to their study.

This selection of texts from a vast range of possibilities (see Appendix for suggestions) is, naturally, restricted by the availability of time and resources. Even the study of television advertisements can become a problem: students may waste hours waiting to record particular examples on video because their next appearance on the screen cannot be predicted. As for the focus of work, and approaches to it, these are partly dictated by age and ability. The more advanced the student, the more sophisticated the analysis and explanation of language data is likely to be. But every project depends in the first place upon the *description* which, at any age, is at the heart of all linguistic study.

The delicacy of these descriptions can increase with students' developing expertise: some of the points made immediately below would not be relevant for younger pupils just getting the feel of language, but they are important in more advanced work.

Description

All the Games have stressed and practised description as the first essential of language work. Section 1 of the Games familiarized students with elements and levels of language that may be described. These include, depending on the focus of the project, phonemes, morphemes, syntactic structures and suprasegmentals, as well as metaphor. The Games in Section 2 practised the recognition and description of contextual variation in these elements. It also introduced students to the significant patterning of discourse.

Fieldwork – collecting data to describe – is at the core of the project. In a sense, it was practised in several of the Games [e.g. **Variety Performance**

2.1] because their role players provided language data for the remainder of the class to consider. Now the field of study is outside the classroom. Tape-recorders and video-cameras can be used in the collection of spoken language as it takes place over the tea-table, in the playground, on the bus, at a party, on the television. Magazines, posters, income tax forms, gardening manuals – all can be discovered in their original, real-life contexts, assembled systematically, their sources carefully recorded. The place of grammar and vocabulary at the heart of human life should become clear and intriguing in the pursuit of original data for original investigation.

However, the collection of data for description can be problematic, not least in its ethics. Harris and Morgan (1979) had some difficulty in explaining to a polytechnic student why he should not first tape the language of his girlfriend when sober, and then get her drunk and compare the results! Whilst most students might have more common sense, it is obviously important to explain, particularly to younger 'researchers', that permission to use sensitive tapes should be sought from the people they wish to record. The same applies to personal written material.

This raises the difficulty of the so-called 'Observer's Paradox', particularly in regard to spoken language. In order to describe it, the researcher obviously needs to hear it! But the presence of the researcher, or merely a tape-recorder, could affect the naturalness of the data. This paradox may have been observed and discussed already: it is possible that the presence of fellow students inhibited participants when playing, for example, **Variety Performance** 2.1.

Teachers will find Wardaugh (1986, esp. chs 6 and 7) helpful in solving this and other difficulties of data collection (see also Stubbs, 1983, particularly for more advanced students). For instance, Wardaugh explains how experienced, professional researchers have tackled similar problems and students can adapt these models for their own purposes. Perhaps one of the best known cautionary tales is research into the language of black teenagers in New York. Investigations, conducted by a white researcher in collar and tie sitting formally on the other side of a table, had tempted so little language from these young people that they were being labelled language*less*. However, when black researchers were involved, over a longish period in informal circumstances, the atmosphere altered: inhibitions were overcome and language flowed, naturally and copi-ously (Labov 1972a). A different approach was taken when Labov wanted to investigate the New York pronunciation of /r/, in words like 'car' and 'cart' (i.e. when it is not occurring, as in 'rat' or 'carry', before a vowel). He chose three stores and simply asked employees where to find a particular item (Labov 1972b: 51). Because his research assistants knew the item was on the *fourth floor*, and as both these words include an /r/ that does not occur before a vowel, responses would be bound to produce plenty of relevant data. And it would be authentic data, since the employees questioned were not inhibited by the knowledge that research was being carried out.[2]

In any event, in whatever way it has been collected, the language brought in from fieldwork will need transcribing on to paper, in a form suitable for description and for sharing with others. Some agreed markers would help here. For instance, language uttered with emphatic stress could be capitalized. If it is exclamatory it could, as in normal writing conventions, be followed by '!', if it is questioning by '?'. If students wish to indicate that they heard a particular tone of voice, they could note it in parentheses beside the utterance, e.g. '(sarcastic)'. A pause of half a second or more could be indicated by three dots. If the pause is less than half a second use two dots. Words that are spoken at the same time as others could be written one utterance above the other and their starting point marked with a square bracket. For example,

Well . . I don't ⎡ think that it?
⎣ But it IS true!

Language that was inaudible could be indicated in parentheses, i.e. '(inaudible)'. Notation for intonation was given in **Sound Sense** (1.7). Different methods of marking the text could be used but, whatever is chosen, students should include an explanatory index.

However, given the limits on project time, not everything can receive meticulous transcription and scrutiny. The complete store data in Labov's experiment might have included, over and above references to the 'fourth floor', extra information about the precise situation of the merchandise. But if these bits of language ('past the suits', 'by the lift', and so on) did not contain examples of the /r/ in which Labov was interested, then – at least by students doing project work – they might be left out of the final transcript. So, in order to prepare a helpfully selective transcript, students must be very clear, before they begin work, about the intended focus of their study.

Being clear about focus, about the kind of context and language to be dealt with, is not of course the same as having an unshakeable conviction, right from the start, about the project's results. The students may be setting out to investigate pre-existing ideas about language but, in the process, they may of course prove, or disprove, their intuitions. Their focus depends upon the investigative questions they want to ask in order to do so.

Perhaps they are interested in the ways with which we ease ourselves into and out of conversations. Students might narrow such an angle down, directing their attention to particular people and/or particular places. They could concentrate, for instance, on the ways in which pupils start talking to each other when they arrive at school in the mornings. Such a project could be tackled by relative beginners to language work, asking simply, of data which might be collected on a tape-recorder installed in the cloakroom:

- What are the first things people in my class say to each other the minute they meet in the mornings?

- What are the very last things they say to each other before they go their separate ways?

Having described their data and so arrived at answers to these questions, young researchers can analyse their discoveries, at least in a general way. They might discuss which kinds of openers and closures are used most, which are used between close friends, which seem to spark off longer conversations, and so on (see next section). More advanced students will naturally address more complex issues.

Analysis

Given the limited time and resources available to them, students will not be able to deal with sufficient data in sufficient depth to be conclusive in their analyses. Still, they can ask interesting questions and arrive at what they will realize are tentative answers. At the very least, these answers must increase their interest in, and respect for, the power of language.

Questions based on *comparison* and *contrast* are good starters for analysis.

With regard to written language, comparison across time might be interesting. Harris and Morgan explain that an older student who insisted on looking at the language of Christmas cards became rapidly bored with their monotony of word and syntactic pattern. If she had thought carefully about an interesting focus for her work at its outset, she might have acquired, from a different historical period, cards that would have added a valuable comparative dimension to her project. The comparison of different kinds of written language is practised in **Shaping Thought** (2.7) and in **Form and Focus** (2.8).

As for spoken language, the comparative analysis of discourse (between cultures, in this case) is practised, albeit in artificial contexts, in **Cross Talk** (2.4), and comparison of dialectal choice is at the root of **Sounds Familiar** (2.2). Comparison, this time of sounds, is also the basis of **Sounds Suspicious** (1.6).

Students wanting to investigate spoken language might develop the work on conversation mentioned above. If, in deliberations about their data, they had wondered about conversation openers and closures between close and not-so-close friends, they will be aware that different kinds of relationships can produce different kinds of language behaviour (something they knew unconsciously but are now making explicit and thus more within their control). More experienced students will be aware that specific variables like, for instance, age, gender or role, may affect the kind of language used. They could therefore decide to limit the collection and description of data to language relating to one or two of these variables. They could choose to concentrate on role, looking at the beginnings of conversations between students and staff as they assemble in the classroom first thing in the morning. They might look at their transcribed data and ask questions like:

- Who speaks first? Is it the person coming into the classroom, or the person already in place?

- Does it make a difference if the person already in the classroom is the student or the teacher?

They could introduce consideration of a second variable and consider whether or not it makes a difference if the student, or the teacher, is male or female.

Alternatively, students might approach their material through a hypothesis. They may have an intuition about language which they wish to check out. It could be something like:

- The person entering the classroom will not speak first, whether or not the person already in the room is a teacher or a student.

Having, through the careful analysis of their descriptions, found answers to their questions, or confirmed or denied their hypotheses, students will want to take their projects a stage further and try to explain the reasons for, and the consequences of, their discoveries.

Explanation

This final stage of the investigation is explanatory. In the case of pupil–teacher communication, project workers might wonder *why* a particular person speaks first, and why this is the same – or different – depending upon precisely who is coming into the room. Their answers could spark interdisciplinary discussion in the language class itself; or maybe their findings could be taken with them for examination in, say, psychology, sociology or history. If, for instance, their teacher always speaks first (and without any specific data this is merely a guess!), does he or she appear to do so for reasons of pedagogy related to control in the classroom? Or is it, though still a matter of control, more to do with hierarchies? Whatever the findings, is it likely they would have been similar in classrooms two or three generations ago? What do students and staff feel are the consequences of the particular routines they adopt?

The older and more advanced the student, the greater the scope for choosing a focus of investigation – description, analysis, explanation – in relation to some clearly articulated theoretical perspective, perhaps based on some previously published research. For instance, A Level students might want to look at conversation openers and closures in relation not only to the variable of role but also of gender. They might want to develop the discussion arising out of **Talking Power** (2.3), describing and analysing any differences they find between male and female communication because they are interested in explaining these in relation to possible power differentials between the sexes. Power and gender is by no means a new peg on which to hang a language discussion so, before they begin their own investigation, students will find plenty to read around the subject [see suggested reading in **Talking Power** (2.3)].

They can then begin their own, original research, choosing to focus their description on specific language features, in relation to specific contexts. They might, for instance, listen out for tag questions in opening and closing exchanges (queries tagged, literally, to the end of statements: 'Nice day, *isn't it?*', 'I hate Mondays, *don't you?*'), analysing the relative amounts and kinds of these used by female and male subjects in a context where there is clear scope for power and control (arguably any and every?).

In their reading, students will have come across the argument that women use tags more than men, particularly in conversation with men, because they are unsure of themselves and want attention and corroboration of their ideas. They will also have seen the alternative suggestion that, whilst some tag uses imply insecurity, others are facilitating, allowing conversations to get going. It is argued that this latter tactic can be a powerful, controlling one – or it can hand the talk over, letting it go to a more dominant partner.

There is clearly room for debate here. But playing the Games will have drawn students' attention to the strong attitudes we all hold towards language in society. They should therefore be on their guard, recognizing their own biases and being ready to adjust their preconceptions as they assess and explain the significance of their original study. The JMB (1987: 7) has as one of its marking criteria 'the open-mindedness with which the investigation has been conducted'.

In this particular project, on tags and gender, students may have to guard against the popular assumption that male use of language is bound to be different and always stronger than female use. For when it comes to assessing and explaining their findings critically, they could well find that women also use their tags powerfully. If so, their study obviously suggests that women can and do use language in similar ways to men. They should then go back to their data and assess precisely *when* women used power language. They will very likely find that women used language powerfully when they were, for some reason, in a powerful position – and men used it weakly when otherwise disadvantaged. Such an observation seems too simple and obvious to be doubted – yet, if students found it to be the case in their experience, it is a point worth making explicit, for some views of female disadvantage are based on what is assumed to be an inevitable linguistic difference and disability *whatever* the context of use.

If the students do reach this kind of conclusion, they may go on to talk about redressing balances, and come to believe that no amount of practising power talk will be effective without the platforms from which to deliver it. If so, their discussion will be demonstrating the interdisciplinary value of linguistics, leading them on to consider, in other classes, the *causes* of women's disadvantage and its manifestations in language.

Project work will have taken them beyond the dispassionate study of invented texts and, through making their findings explicit, it will have emphasized the power and limitations of language as it is used in the real world, drawing students to consider the relationship of real language with other aspects of their real lives.

Such an outcome might seem sufficient in itself. However, in this real world, grades are to be achieved, examinations passed. The following section, therefore, makes some suggestions about the assessment of project work.

Assessment

General remarks

There are several aspects of project work that can be assessed. Accuracy of description, which uses a metalanguage suited to the age and ability of the student, is of course essential for the success of the whole project. But, in addition, the effectiveness of data collection, its transcription and its presentation may be marked. Perceptiveness and judgement in analysis and explanation will obviously be of particular account in the case of older students.

If required, the personal skills necessary for project work (involving independence, organization, management and communication) can be assessed indirectly from the success of the finished product. But grading and commenting on these practical elements will be easier if a student keeps a project diary, outlining behind-the-scenes work – its difficulties as well as its achievements.

Presentation skills are an optional extra in projects. But if students can explain their research to their peers, a great deal of original work can be shared. The quality of written and oral material presented to the class may be graded according to its clarity and accessibility, but obviously some students find the task stressful and inhibiting. They would much prefer to settle for an essay written and marked in privacy. However, the role playing and group-based work that is at the core of the language Games should help prepare students for the challenges of presentation before an audience. There is obviously an opportunity for peer group assessment here, but many students find marking their friends difficult and disconcerting. Involving them closely in the establishment of clear grading criteria helped us to some extent, and the habit of close monitoring, practised by observers of role plays during the Games, can help students to see the task more objectively.

The Games, based as they are on group work, can also pave the way for *team* projects. Team work is clearly not an option at A Level, but it has advantages which may be worth considering at other stages. Its assessment, however, does present special difficulties.

Team work and its assessment: 'Pros and cons'

The 'pros'

We chose to do linguistic projects at The Nottingham Trent University in groups of fours, partly because we assumed that more fieldwork could be accomplished in a group, and because combined effort might extend the scope and sophistication of the investigation. Our optimism proved well-founded. One group wanted to look at the playground language of children and having a team of four researchers meant that, despite our limited time-scale, a variety of schools and a variety of ages could be recorded ready for group discussion: one person working alone could not have collected so much data, and scope for comparative analysis would have been limited. Another group wanted to investigate the relative success of different interview techniques. Each team member observed a different series of interviews and made her preliminary observations, but it was not until she was able to compare and contrast these in debate with her colleagues that it became very clear what kinds of discourse constituted, in the collective judgement of this team, a 'successful' interview.

In general, the students shared our faith in the team approach. Besides, group work is a natural extension of the Games we played from time to time during the course, for these frequently work as team efforts. One student on a Communication Studies course remarked, 'Teamwork is essential: that's what this course should be about. You can only go so far in communicating with books!'

As for ourselves, projects require a lot of staff support if they are to go beyond the superficial and we should not have had the time needed to advise our large number of students individually in this kind of exercise. For us, quite apart from what we believe are its considerable advantages, project work has to be in teams or not at all.

We also felt that skills of communication, organization, cooperation and commitment, and of adapting to the different talents and levels of ability in colleagues (all of which are called for in team work) must stand the students in good stead for life after their degree course – and, for that matter, during it. At first, students whose courses had not involved this sort of operation before expressed considerable anxiety and annoyance. Individual team members' bus timetables, class timetables, social timetables, all, they argued, hindered getting together for joint work. But, having accepted that we did not consider it our responsibility to sort these matters out for them, the mood improved and feedback became positive. Some felt they did more work because others were relying on them. One remarked, 'It's good to organize yourself round other people and to consider their views and choices.' Another said, 'The main reason I think some people had difficulty coming to terms with the concept of team work is that education in general suffers from a chronic dose of competitiveness – something I think team work can go some way to reducing.' Another, training to be a teacher, thought that working 'alongside other students of different abilities and experiencing the problems of this is very useful'.

Nevertheless, some students still found team work very stressful. However, we had stopped formal teaching one month before the end of the course and given four weeks class time to advising the groups. Because each had chosen a very different project, none of them precisely following one of the course

lectures, this was essential in order to give every project the individual attention it needed. But it also gave us time to support those who were having most
difficulty getting started and working together. At the end of the exercise,
these groups had, on the whole, gained in confidence and were pleased with
themselves for coping with a difficult task.

Still, the exercise was not without headaches!

The 'cons'

Because we were working with teams, we feel that we had more time to give
careful assessment and feedback: marking and commenting on one project,
though each was considerably longer than one essay, took us less time than
four individual pieces of work.

However, we wanted to reward not only the end-product of the project but
also the team work that had gone into it. We take Graham Gibbs's (1990: 7)
point that assessing members' performance of specific team tasks – like chairing
team meetings, managing individual and team time, negotiating smoothly –
may not be so important as judging

> ... students' ability to recognise team problems when they see them, diagnose
> them, act to do something about them, and check whether the new way of
> operating is working. It may be this active effort to try to improve which has
> more impact than the use of any specific technique or behaviour. This is a more
> dynamic and forward-looking view of teamwork.

In order to get some sense of the teams' problem-solving capacities, we met all
of them a number of times during their month of project work. On these
occasions, we could get an idea of the ways in which difficulties were being
faced and resolved. We also asked the groups to keep diaries that documented
the pitfalls they encountered and explained how they tackled them.

However, if the development of team work is itself a prime objective of
project work, then Gibbs's proposal for an examination question, encouraging
students to recognize the importance of the exercise, is surely worth following.
Gibbs suggests (1990: 9):

> Use an exam question of the form: Give an account of the way your team strove
> to operate effectively. What general issues emerged about the operation of teams?
> What steps might you personally take to address these issues next time you work
> in a team? You can even warn students in advance that they will get such an exam
> question – the only way they can revise for it is to reflect on the operation of their
> team and find out more about explanations and alternatives!

So much for the team as a whole. However, the students were reading for
individual degrees. They naturally wished to succeed as individuals and,
therefore, although we wanted them to have the experience and advantages of
team cooperation, we also felt we should be able to give each one individual

feedback and assessment. But how to tell who had done what, when and how successfully.

Again, the diary helped. The students logged each individual effort. At least, they recorded who collected this bit of fieldwork, who did this bit of background reading, who did the typing up, and so on. So we had a fair idea of how the spade work had been shared out. But, apart from mentioning who had read which book, there were rarely any clues in the diaries as to who had the *ideas*. It was also impossible to judge this from the finished project. As it was supposed to be a group effort, a student did not sign a particular section even if he or she had been directly responsible for it.

In the end, we decided on an element of peer group assessment, following a tried and tested scheme from the Engineering Department. Each team member had 100 marks to divide, in any proportion they thought fit, between their three co-workers (giving none to themselves). The students were to give brief reasons for their chosen distribution. We tallied up the marks per person, moved the decimal point two places, and used it as a factor with which to multiply the team mark. If the team mark was 60 per cent and one member has totalled 90 marks from their team, he or she would receive a mark of $60 \times 0.9 = 54.0$.[3] In fact, unlike engineering students who register striking variations in their percentages, most of our groups chose to award equal marks to each of their participants. Besides, they were apparently rewarding effort – even though we had discussed marking criteria with the whole class before they made their decisions – and so we were no nearer to discovering and acknowledging individual intellectual contributions. Next time we are considering returning projects with our comments, and with a team mark, before asking the students to record their peer scores and then give them back to us for final, individual, grading. This way each group will know which part of their project has been most successful, in our judgement, and they may be better placed to assess their co-workers' intellectual input.[4]

In general, our students produced good work, within the usual curve of grades. However, it was interesting that some who, by the second year, were known as 'good' students (i.e. particularly able to cope with theoretical aspects of their course) did not do specially well: their fieldwork and its description were poorly done, so their analysis and explanatory work were ill-founded. Conversely, some who were not highly rated, in this sort of way, produced original and intelligent work. The reason behind the 'good' students' disappointing performance could *not* be that projects do not require a theoretical understanding. On the contrary, understanding theory is a pre-condition of the work at all its stages. It may be – but this can only be speculation until we have more experience of linguistic project work – that the 'good' students were not only reluctant to set books aside for a while but also, perhaps more significantly, were not always willing to challenge their favourite theories in the field. Similarly (though, again, this is only conjecture), it may be that the 'less good' did well because they came to terms with theory through testing it out in practice – and, moreover, in a practice which was non-threatening because it is in no way esoteric.

If these tentative explanations are borne out in future years, they would seem to be more good evidence in favour of using experiential methods in the teaching of language. Playing the language game can, at all ages, be both encouraging and challenging for students with different abilities and with different interests. For though language is the stuff of everyday life, its experience in the controlled framework of games or of projects, particularly those accomplished in groups, can enable, as Warner Weil and McGill argue (with regard to all kinds of experiential learning) 'the discovery of possibilities that may not be evident from direct experience alone'. For participants must '*purposefully* reflect upon, validate, transform, give personal meaning to and seek to integrate their different ways of knowing' (Warner Weil and McGill 1989: 248).

Appendix to Chapter 4

Suggestions – from an infinite list of possibilities – for project texts and themes.

1 *Written texts*
  posters
  adverts
  appliance instructions
  games instructions
  notices on student boards
  editorials
  newspaper headlines
  comics and magazines
  official forms
  cookery books
  travel journalism
  holiday sales brochures
  art reviews
  theatre/concert programmes
  school reports
  school exercise books
  exam papers

2 *Spoken language texts and contexts*
  media chat shows
  political broadcasting
  news reports
  weather reports
  games shows
  sports commentaries

doctor to patient language
employer to employee language
interviews
teacher to pupil language
class/tutorial/seminar/lecture language
the language of mothers to daughters and sons
the language of fathers to daughters and sons
male/female teachers talking to male/female students
children at particular ages
dialects

3 *Sample ideas from some of our first-year polytechnic project groups*
Astrology forecasts from different magazines compared.
Letters from an adult to a friend compared with those from a child to the same friend.
Comparison of British and American chat show hosts' language.
Comparison of news bulletins on Radio 1 and Radio 4.
Comparison of television health and safety adverts apparently geared to different audiences.
The language in modern-day magazine adverts and in those of previous decades.
Description and analysis of credit card advertisements.
Comparison of political leaders' language during interviews.
A political leader's language when interviewed compared with the language the same person used on a Party Political Broadcast.
A poem written in Non-standard English compared with the same writer's 'translation' of this into Standard English.
The language of (the British) 'The Bill' compared with that of (the American) 'Hawaii Five-O'.

4 *Notes with regard to our second-year groups*
Second years, as individuals, are required to take a linguistic issue and discuss it theoretically, in an essay, before teaming up with others to re-search a topic arising out of this issue. Many of these students are drawn to work in the language and gender area and have re-run – to a limited extent, of course, bearing in mind our time and resource restrictions – small research projects they have read about during the year. For example, how long, in comparison with previous studies, do the students find that men and women talk in response to a question asking for an opinion?

Discussion of the language of autistic people, and of others with language disability, takes place in the second year and students have wanted to re-search these areas. However, we have not encouraged them to do so because there are difficult ethical issues involved in collecting relevant data and students need a special expertise in interviewing which is beyond the scope of our course.

Notes to Chapter 4

1 Similar stages are specifically required for the London Board A Level project but the word 'description' is used in a slightly different sense in the 1991–92 examination syllabus.
2 Permission to record responses would, presumably, not have been ethically necessary because the anonymity of the speakers could be maintained in this study.
3 It should be explained to students, so that they do not skew final marks completely out of proportion, that if their peer marks produce widely divergent factors within a team, then the final group scores will be very broadly spread – perhaps unrealistically.
4 We are also asking for individually written essays from our students who have to produce more than one piece of coursework for us in the year. We want this essay to discuss the theoretical background to an aspect of linguistics. Students will then join up for project work with others who have been interested in the same topic and together they will choose a project arising out of it. This scheme will give students a chance to show what they can do on their own as well as in teams and also ensures that they are well grounded in background before they undertake their research.

Afterword

In the classroom language game there are no penalties and everyone shares the prize: an explicit understanding of the real-life 'game' and its players.

Bibliography

Aitchison, J. (1987) *Teach Yourself Linguistics*, 3rd edn. Sevenoaks, Hodder and Stoughton.

Aitchison, J. (1989) *The Articulate Mammal*, 3rd edn. London, Unwin Hyman.

Austin, J.L. (1962) *How to Do Things with Words*. New York, Oxford University Press.

Bain, R. (1991) *Reflection: Talking about Language*. Sevenoaks, Hodder and Stoughton.

Baldwin, J. and French, P. (1990) *Forensic Phonetics*. London, Pinter.

Berlin, B. and Kay, P. (1969) *Basic Color Terms: Their Universality and Evolution*. Berkeley, University of California Press.

Birch, D. (1989) *Language, Literature and Critical Practice*. London, Routledge.

Blake, N.F. (1990) *An Introduction to the Language of Literature*. London, Macmillan.

Brown, G. (1990) Walking and talking. *Critical Quarterly*, Winter, 32 (4): 34–8.

Bullock, Sir Alan (1975) *A Language for Life*. London, HMSO.

Burton, D. (1980) *Dialogue and Discourse*. London, Routledge and Kegan Paul.

Cameron, D. (1985) *Feminism and Linguistic Theory*. London, Macmillan.

Cameron, D. (ed.) (1991) *The Feminist Critique of Language*. London, Routledge.

Cameron, D. and Bourne, J. (1989) Nation and citizenship: Kingman in linguistic and historical perspective. *Department of English and Media Studies Occasional Papers*, No. 1. Institute of Education, University of London.

Carroll, J.B. (ed.) (1956) *Language, Thought and Reality: Selected Writings of Benjamin Lee Whorf*. Cambridge and New York, MIT Press and John Wiley.

Carroll, L. (1958) *Alice's Adventures In Wonderland*, and *Through the Looking Glass*. London, Macmillan (first published 1865, 1872).

Carter, R. (1982) *Language and Literature: An Introductory Reader in Stylistics*. London, Allen and Unwin.

Carter, R. and Simpson, P. (eds) (1988) *Language, Discourse and Literature*. London, Unwin Hyman.

Chomsky, N. (1959) Review of Skinner's *Verbal Behavior*. *Language*, 35, 26–58.

Coates, J. (1986) *Women, Men and Language*. New York, Longman.

Coates, J. and Cameron, D. (eds) (1988) *Women in Their Speech Communities*. London, Longman.

Cox, B. (1991) *Cox on Cox*. Sevenoaks, Hodder and Stoughton.

Crystal, D. (1988) *Rediscover Grammar with David Crystal*. London, Longman.

Daly, M. (1978) *Gyn/Ecology: The Metaethics of Radical Feminism.* Boston, Beacon Press.

Department of Education and Science and the Welsh Office (1990) *English in the National Curriculum, No. 2.* London, HMSO.

Deucher, M. (1984) *British Sign Language.* London, Routledge and Kegan Paul.

Doughty, P., Lushington, S., Pearce, J., Thornton, G. and Wood, K. (1969) *Language in Use: Schools Council Programme in Linguistics and English Teaching, 16+ Trial Material.* University College London, The Schools Council Publications Co. Ltd.

Doughty, P., Pearce, J. and Thornton, G. (1971) *Language in Use.* London, Edward Arnold.

Fairclough, N. (1989) *Language and Power.* London, Longman.

Firmage, G.J. (1981) *e.e. cummings, Complete Poems 1910–1962.* London, Granada.

Fiske, J. (1982) *Introduction to Communication Studies.* London, Methuen.

Flower, F.D. (1966) *Language and Education.* London, Longmans, Green and Co. Ltd.

Fowler, R., Hodge, H., Kress, G. and Trew, T. (1979) *Language and Control.* London, Routledge and Kegan Paul.

Fromkin, V. and Rodman, R. (1988) *An Introduction to Language,* 4th edn. Fort Worth, Holt, Rinehart and Winston.

Gardner, W.H. (ed.) (1953) *Gerard Manley Hopkins: Poems and Prose.* Harmondsworth, Penguin.

Gibbs, G. (1990) Assessing teamwork skills. *Bulletin of Teaching and Learning,* 5, Autumn, pp. 6–9.

Goffman, E. (1976) Replies and responses. *Language in Society,* 5: 257–313.

Grice, H.P. (1975) Logic and conversation. In P. Cole and J. Morgan (eds) *Syntax and Semantics, III: Speech Acts.* New York, Academic Press.

Gumperz, J.J. and Hymes, D. (eds) (1972) *Directions in Sociolinguistics: The Ethnography of Communications.* New York, Holt, Rinehart and Winston.

Halliday, M.A.K. (1973) *Explorations in the Functions of Language.* London, Edward Arnold.

Halliday, M.A.K. (1975) *Learning How to Mean.* London, Edward Arnold.

Halliday, M.A.K. (1985) *An Introduction to Functional Grammar.* London, Edward Arnold.

Harris, W. and Morgan, K. (1979) *Language Projects: An Introduction to the Study of Language.* London, Edward Arnold.

Haynes, J. (1989) *Introducing Stylistics.* London, Unwin Hyman.

Hockett, C. and Altmann, S. (1968) A note on design features. In T. Sebeok (ed.) *Animal Communication: Techniques of Study and Results of Research.* Bloomington, Ind., Indiana University Press.

Hodge, R. and Kress, G. (1988) *Social Semiotics.* Cambridge, Polity Press.

Honey, J. (1989) *Does Accent Matter? The Pygmalion Factor.* London, Faber and Faber.

Hymes, D. (1971) *On Communicative Competence.* Philadelphia, University of Pennsylvania Press.

Hymes, D. (1977) *Foundations in Sociolinguistics: An Ethnographic Approach.* London, Tavistock.

Joint Matriculation Board (1987) *Instructions and Guidance for Teachers.* Manchester, JMB.

Jones, B. (1962) *The Poems of William Barnes,* 2 vols. Sussex, Centaur Press.

Jones, K. (1987) *Simulations. A Handbook for Teachers and Trainers*, 2nd edn. London, Kegan Page.

Katriel, T. (1986) *Talking Straight: Dugri Speech in Israeli Sabra Culture.* Cambridge, Cambridge University Press.

Kingman, Sir John (1988) *Report of the Committee of Inquiry into the Teaching of English.* London, HMSO.

Klima, E. and Bellugi, U. (1979) *The Signs of Language.* Cambridge, Mass., Harvard University Press.

Kress, G.R. and Hodge, R. (1979) *Language as Ideology.* London, Routledge and Kegan Paul.

Labov, W. (1972a) *Language in the Inner City: Studies in the Black English Vernacular.* Philadelphia, University of Pennsylvania Press.

Labov, W. (1972b) *Sociolinguistic Patterns.* Philadelphia, University of Pennsylvania Press.

Ladefoged, P. (1982) *A Course in Phonetics*, 2nd edn. New York, Harcourt Brace Jovanovich.

Lakoff, G. and Johnson, M. (1980) *Metaphors We Live By.* Chicago, University of Chicago Press.

Leonard, T. (1984) *Intimate Voices: Selected Work 1965–1983.* Newcastle upon Tyne, Galloping Dog Press.

Leonard, T. (1987) Interview. *Edinburgh Review*, 77: 40–48, 59–72.

Lyons, J. (1991) *Chomsky*, 3rd edn. London, Fontana.

Malinowski, B. (1923) The problem of meaning in primitive languages. In C.K. Ogden and I.A. Richards (eds) *The Meaning of Meaning.* London, Routledge and Kegan Paul.

Mercer, N. (ed.) (1988) *Language and Literacy from an Educational Perspective, Vol. 1: Language Studies.* Milton Keynes, Open University Press.

Miles, E. (1988) *British Sign Language.* London, BBC Books.

Montague, J. (ed.) (1974) *The Faber Book of Irish Verse.* London, Faber and Faber.

Montgomery, M. (1985) *Introduction to Language and Society.* London, Methuen.

Morley, G.D. (1985) *An Introduction to Systemic Grammar.* London, Macmillan.

Nash, W. (1985) *The Language of Humour: Style and Technique in Comic Discourse.* London, Longman.

National Curriculum Council (1989) *Consultation Report: English 5–11 in the National Curriculum.* York, National Curriculum Council.

Norwich, J.J. (1982) *Christmas Crackers.* Harmondsworth, Penguin.

O'Barr, W. and Atkins, B. (1980) 'Women's language' or 'powerless language'? In S. McConnell-Ginet, R. Borker and N. Furman (eds) *Women and Language in Literature and Society*, pp. 93–110. New York, Praeger.

Pierce, C.S. (1931–58) *Collected Papers.* Cambridge, Mass., Harvard University Press.

Ricks, C. (1969) *The Poems of Tennyson.* London, Longman.

Roach, P. (1991) *English Phonetics and Phonology*, 2nd edn. Cambridge, Cambridge University Press.

Sapir, B.L. (1921) *Language: An Introduction to the Study of Speech.* New York, Harcourt, Brace and World.

Scott, P. (1989) *Reconstructing 'A' Level English.* Milton Keynes, Open University Press.

Searle, J. (1969) *Speech Acts: An Essay in the Philosophy of Language.* Cambridge, Cambridge University Press.

Secretary of State for Education and Science and the Secretary of State for Wales (1989) *Proposals for English for ages 5 to 16*. London, Department of Education and Science and the Welsh Office.

Shepherd, V. (1990) *Language Variety and the Art of the Everyday*. London, Pinter.

Shepherd, V. (forthcoming) *Literature about Language*. London, Routledge.

Sinclair, J. McH. and Coulthard, R.M. (1975) *Towards an Analysis of Discourse: The English Used by Teachers and Pupils*. Oxford, Oxford University Press.

Skinner, B.F. (1957) *Verbal Behaviour*. New York, Appleton-Century-Croft.

Sontag, S. (1989) *AIDS and Its Metaphors*. Harmondsworth, Penguin.

Stubbs, M. (1983) *Discourse Analysis: The Sociolinguistic Analysis of Natural Language*. Oxford, Basil Blackwell.

Sutcliffe, D. and Wong, A. (eds) (1986) *The Language of the Black Experience*. Oxford, Basil Blackwell.

Taylor, J. and Walford, R. (1978) *Learning and the Simulation Game*, 2nd edn. Milton Keynes, Open University Press.

Traugott, E.C. and Pratt, M.L. (1980) *Linguistics for Students of Literature*. New York, Harcourt Brace Jovanovich.

Trudgill, P. (1975) *Accent, Dialect and the School*. London, Edward Arnold.

Trudgill, P. (1983) *Sociolinguistics: An Introduction to Language and Society*. Harmondsworth, Penguin.

Wardaugh, R. (1985) *How Conversation Works*. Oxford, Basil Blackwell.

Wardaugh, R. (1986) *An Introduction to Sociolinguistics*. Oxford, Basil Blackwell.

Warner Weil, S. and McGill, I. (eds) (1989) *Making Sense of Experiential Learning*: *Diversity in Theory and Practice*. Milton Keynes, The Society for Research into Higher Education and Open University Press.

Williams, E. (ed.) (1967) *An Anthology of Concrete Poetry*. New York, Something Else Press.

Williams, E. (1992) *My Life in Flux – and Vice Versa*. London, Thames and Hudson.

Wood, V. (1985) *Up To You, Porky: The Victoria Wood Sketch Book*. London, Methuen.

Index